100

Full Gospel

Bible Stories

Valerie Jensen Gibson

Foreword

All honor and praise goes first and foremost to God our Father in Heaven, God the Son, Jesus who reaches down to us, and God the Holy Spirit who dwells among us and in us. Secondly, I would like to express my deepest gratitude to Pastor Jack Sipe Sr. of Faith Outreach Church in Middletown, Pennsylvania.

A former U.S. Marine and 7th degree black belt in the art of Isshin Ryu Karate, Pastor Jack diligently continues his daily study of the Bible, always with an open mind to receive new revelations from the Holy Spirit. This disciplined endeavor has spanned three decades. At the age of 77, he continues to be a full time Pastor of Faith Outreach Church.

Many of the poems in this book were created directly from Pastor Jack's sermons. Others were inspired by his teachings. Therefore, if anyone has pertinent theological questions regarding these poems, please pose them to the same humble expert on whom I rely, Pastor Jack Sipe.

The inspiration for *The Big Picture* is "Betrayed!" by Stan Telchin. Early in my Christian walk, I learned so much about Christianity and its roots in Judaism from this excellent book. E.W. Kenyon's "The Father and His Family" is invaluable to new Christians. Chapter four gives an eye-opening description of the devil, and is the source for the poem, *God is Not in Control*. "Practicing His Presence," a collection of the works of two beautiful men of God; Brother Lawrence and Frank Laubach, is the source for the poem *Practicing His Presence*. "Alcoholics Anonymous" contains a program that works because it teaches its' victims to depend on God. *We "Agnostics"* is based on chapter four of this wonderful book. And last but not least, about our future in Christ, is *Heaven and Earth*; based on Dr. Randy Alcorn's all-encompassing, scripture-based book, "Heaven."

God bless you all, in Jesus' name.

Valerie Jensen Gibson

Contents

Contents

Contents

Contents

1 *God's Own System of Justice*

Though the Bible does not clearly indicate God has His own
Set of rules He must follow, one need not look hard to be shown.
It is obvious that He has boundaries that He does obey.
The beginning is where we will start; with creation's last day.

In six days God created all heaven and earth, seas and land
And all animals. In His own image created He man.
On the seventh day God rested from all His work which He made.
And He never created again. His own "rule" He obeyed.

Once created He Adam, then Eve from his rib God did make.
And consider that when Adam sinned, God did not him forsake.
God did not discard Adam and start again with a new man.
Knowing that he would fall, man's redemption was already planned.

When God finally did destroy most of mankind with the flood,
Only Noah, three sons and their wives in an ark made of wood
From destruction were saved, along with all the creatures of earth.
Why did God not start over? Instead He did plan our new birth.

See when Satan caused Adam to sin against God with a lie,
This sin nature consumed Adam's soul, and his spirit did die.
God's creation was severed from God who Himself is unstained.
All inherit this curse, and in Satan's control earth remains.

Thus when Jesus took on a flesh body, it could not be from
The corrupt seed of Adam. We needed His body to come
From the seed of a woman conceived by God's own Holy Ghost,
To be free from the curse of the fall, for to save all the lost.

So this battle had started between God and Satan who hates
All God's children, for whom God did make a way to vindicate.
Adam's lease on this earth, which then Satan did steal, expires when
Our Lord Jesus returns. Satan reigns on this earth until then.

So you see God cannot, by His own rules, make Satan depart.
For God plays by the rules, but He made us a way if we're smart.
Revelation tells of Satan's future and where he will go.
But while Satan's still free to deceive, there are things we should know.

Jesus Christ is the second man Adam who lived without sin.
Romans five explains how by His death on the cross He did win
Back our righteousness. Thus He redeemed us to God by His grace.
By accepting God's free gift, our Saviour we'll see face to face.

2 *Evicted*

I've heard it said that God cannot be in the presence of
A sinner; that's the reason Eve and Adam God did shove
Out of the Garden, Eden. All one has to do is read
The Bible to acknowledge, "That's not true." There was a need.

For one thing, you can see that God still talked to sinners for
A long time after Eve and Adam were expelled. Be sure
To notice after Cain did kill his brother, Abel, he
Conversed with God in Genesis 4:9 to 4:16.

And also notice, "Cain went from the presence of the Lord..."
So *Cain left* God. But back to Adam... God could not afford
To let His fallen children, Eve and Adam, thus remain
In Eden in their fallen state, to live forever shamed.

In Genesis 3:22 God said, "Behold, the man
(He) is become as one of *us*..." (God in three Persons) and
Now knowing good and evil, lest he take of this life tree
"...And eat, and live for ever:" from the garden he must leave.

If Adam, he had eaten from the Tree of Life, then he
Would live forever in his fallen state. There'd never be
The chance for a Redeemer, Jesus. Satan would have won.
But we are both redeemed and righteous, thanks to God's own Son.

3 *Born Losers*

The most difficult truth to conceive, for a Christian, is why
The Lord Jesus as our Substitute on that cross had to die.
Why was this unavoidable? Wasn't there some other way?
Let us see why this had to be done to redeem us that day.

If one looks back before there was time, to what little we know
Of the spiritual world, in Isaiah 14 it does show
In verse twelve to fourteen just how Satan desired to be like
God Himself. And so Lucifer down, for his pride, God did strike.

In the twenty-eighth part of Ezekiel, also we see
Some more verses describing the devil, particularly
Verses thirteen through nineteen. These tell why he fell from God's
grace.
And they tell of his future. This battle between, we now face.

And the other thing we must consider is limits God set
On Himself. Although He can do anything, He does not let
Himself go against His "Constitution;" His system of how
Things should be. For His justice and judgment are truths He allows.

For example, when Adam rebelled, God did not wipe him out
And start over. Created He once, and He is not about
To go back on this limit He set on Himself. If one needs
Further proof of this fact then just read about Noah, indeed.

For God went to the trouble to have Noah build a great ark,
To save all the land animals, plus Noah's family. Stark
Was God's dealing with man, wiping most off the face of the earth.
But let's backtrack to Adam and show what to God man is worth.

God commanded of Adam in Genesis 2 that he may
Of all trees in the garden, but one, eat the fruit. So God gave
Adam choice. And in Genesis 3 Adam fell, for he chose
His wife Eve over God. From his spirit God's life he did lose.

There's a quote from "The Shack," (a great book!) that says man did declare
Independence from God when that choice Adam made. Be aware,
In this battle between God and Satan, just pawns are we. When
Satan tricked God's creation, he seized man's authority then.

Now no longer could God enter man by his spirit. God lost
Direct access to man. Satan stole this approach, and the cost
To God's children was darkness inside, in our spirits. This death
All inherit from Adam. Born losers are we from first breath.**

First Corinthians 15 verse twenty-one and twenty-two
Show us God's Constitution. By man came our death, and so too
Must salvation from death come by man. But how could this be done
When all men were corrupted from Adam? The answer's God's Son.

As in Adam all die, even so in Christ all are made live.
Thus the incorrupt seed of a woman, as God did contrive,
Was conceived by the Holy Ghost; not by the seed of a man.
So from birth God was in Jesus' spirit. We'd say "born again."

How do we become winners? We're "born again" when we believe
In Lord Jesus, who paid the steep price, and His life we receive.
Now God lives in our spirits. This free gift we pay nothing for.
For it cannot be earned, nor deserved; just accepted. No more.

One more thing to consider. Once God lives in you, don't stop there.
For your mind can now learn from your Spirit. Seek Him. Be aware,
You can still be deceived by the devil, like Eve, even though
She had God's life within her. She lost Him. We can't. Good to know.

**Now this story sounds neat, but there is a *correction* that must
Be included. Like Pastor Jack says, "If you're wrong, then the just
Thing to do is admit it." This story's misleading, for no
One is *born* a "born loser." We're all of us born with His glow.

John 1:9 tells us Jesus, He is the true Light, and he lights
Every man who comes into the world. And His light, this is Life
In our spirits. So babies aborted, and those who die young
Go to be with their Father in Heaven. Their song's not unsung.

There's a moment in everyone's life they're accountable. Then
They must choose in their heart to believe, or to not. This is when
They remain with God's life (or His light) in their spirit. Or they
Decide they don't believe, and their spirit gets dark on that day.

Now the Bible does not give an age that's specific when one
Must decide to believe, or to not. But God gave us His Son,
Jesus Christ. John 1:18 says Jesus, He came to reveal
Father God to us all. Father wants kids who love Him for real.

4 God's Mercy

Now have you ever wondered why things happened quite the way
they did?
Why just one act of disobedience on Adam's part did rid
Him of the right to live in Paradise with Eve. And also they
Did lose their fellowship with God. Their spirits truly died that day.

Well we must look behind the scenes to understand the devil's role.
His hate for God was lashed out on Creation. Adam's reign he stole.
In Genesis and three we see how Satan did deceive these two.
Like stealing candy from a baby; babes they were. Their lives were
new.

Now one may think 'tis awful that God forced them out of Eden. He
Did not want them to eat now from the Tree of Life, for they would
be
Eternally indebted then to Satan. They'd forever live
Disgraced with the sin nature their forbidden act of wrong did give.

God knew that they would fall. In verse fifteen He told them of His
plan
To thus redeem Creation to Himself. To earth He'd send a Man;
A second Adam as described in Romans chapter five, His Son.
And so began the story of six thousand years. His work is done.

Two thousand years ago the Second Adam, Jesus, He became
A man. He took on flesh and lived an earthly life like us. The same
Temptations He did face as we, but still no sin did He employ.
The cross made all the difference. Satan's power of death He did
destroy.

So what about the souls who died before the Lord did save us from
A spiritual death imposed by Satan? For the Lord did come
Four thousand years then after Adam. Countless millions died without
A Saviour. But a second chance they got, and took it; there's no doubt.

For when the Lord descended into hell after succumbing to
His death upon the cross for all the sins of man, the penance due
He paid. Three days He spent in hell and preached to all the captives
there,
And brought them out of hell when He ascended out of Satan's lair.

One really can't imagine there was anyone who stayed behind
In hell. All saints and sinners were redeemed to Father God in kind.
For every sin and sickness that man has, or had, or that will be,
God put on Him. We're covered by His blood for all eternity.

The only "catch" that now exists for anyone to thus receive
This gift of free salvation from the Lord is only to believe
That Jesus died for us, that He's God's Son, and that He rose again.
John 1 verse twelve says when we do this, we are sons of God. Amen!

5 Why Egypt?

The whole world knows the Israelites' story of how they were brought
Out of bondage in Egypt through miracles God Himself wrought.
Through God's might, not their own, they did make an astounding retreat.
These were God's chosen people. Their enemies God did defeat.

God sent Moses, His servant, to Pharaoh to ask him to free
All the Hebrews. But God said Himself Pharaoh would not agree.
For God hardened his heart; several times it's in Exodus shown.
God through plagues and disasters unspeakable made Himself known.

He turned rivers to blood. He sent frogs, swarms of flies and then slew
All the cattle of Egypt, then sent again Moses unto
Pharaoh's presence to make His announcement in Exodus 9,
Verses thirteen through sixteen. A purpose God had for these signs.

For His name was declared then throughout all the earth. And His own
Chosen people would say that He IS the "I AM" they did know
To deliver them. All that the hail and the fire did not void
Of its land, then the locusts did eat leaving Egypt destroyed.

Pharaoh begged and the Lord then removed all the locusts, but still
He would not let the children of Israel go, not until
There was darkness most dreadful, and after that Pharaoh would let
Them go, but, just their people, not cattle. The worst would come yet.

By the blood of a lamb on their doorways, the Israelites got
From the last plague protected. All firstborn were smote who did not
Have this blood them to cover. This first of "Passovers" would be
Now remembered forever by Jews as the night God them freed.

The Egyptians were horrified. They urged the Hebrews "Be Gone."
Clothed and ready they'd been. They all made their retreat before
dawn,
Bearing jewels of both gold and of silver, and raiment. They gained
Everything they required, plus good health. Not one feeble remained.

Moses led them through wilderness such as did fringe the Red Sea.
In a pillar of cloud by the day, fire by night God did lead
Them. The fight was not over, but it was God's battle, for He
The Egyptians hearts hardened again. They pursued to the Sea.

Then spectacularly, Moses stretched out his hand and the Lord
Caused the Sea to be split with two walls. On dry ground did the
horde
Of the Israelites cross the Red Sea. The Egyptians went in
After them and were drowned when the turbulent Sea closed again.

Look once more at Passover. The blood of a lamb did secure
The Jews' fate. Thus a preview of Jesus this was to be sure.
John the Baptist called Jesus the "Lamb of God, which takes away
(All) the sin of the world;" in John 1:29 he did say.

First Corinthians 5 and verse seven, Paul says about He,
Jesus "Christ our Passover is sacrificed for us" we see.
His shed blood on the cross did redeem us to God. It makes one
Tremble when we see how all God did points to Jesus, His Son.

Before Exodus, only a handful of people on earth
Were aware of God's presence and greatness. A spiritual birth
Is what He was preparing for us, from the Garden unto
His Son's death on the cross. Jesus Christ's sacrifice makes us new.

6 *The Big Picture*

The Israelites thought the Messiah would be
A great king who would free them from all tyranny,
And that they would become a great nation again
Like they were in the days of the wise Solomon.

So when Jesus was born as a babe who'd be king,
Most did not comprehend that their Saviour would bring
To them peace as described in Philippians 4
And verse 7, and all of the gospels and more.

Thus this peace, it was not as most Jews did expect.
For their thinking was smaller. They did not suspect
That their God had a plan that would set all men free.
It began in verse 15 of Genesis 3.

In Genesis 3 is when Satan deceived
God's creation and stole life from Adam and Eve.
The transference was legal and their spirits died.
Though their bodies kept living, from God they were pried.

But the Jews we must realize followed God's plan;
And from Abraham on they had started a clan
Of God's people. And knowing not why they were made
To keep themselves separate, their God they obeyed.

Looking back we can see that God's purpose for this
Separation was so He could limit access
To His people from Satan who poisons our lives.
Look what happened to Solomon when he chose wives

From the world and their cultures they brought with them too,
Thus infecting God's people and Solomon knew
That his heart had been turned from his God and he made
Lamentations to God of his youth he'd betrayed.

More importantly though were the records they kept
Of their census recording their lineage in depth.
Thus from David the King did Lord Jesus descend,
Showing He is Messiah the Father did send.

If Messiah has yet to arrive as some claim,
Then the proof of His lineage no longer remains.
For the temple destroyed was in 70 A.D.,
And this prophecy of the Messiah is key.

It took four thousand years for God's plan to complete,
To take back what was stolen by Satan's deceit.
For in Genesis 3 verse 15 God did tell
Of Jesus our Saviour who'd save us from hell.

If Satan had understood what God had meant,
Never would he have touched our Lord Jesus God sent.
The atonement He made for us all with His blood
Would replace now forever Passover for good.

When we choose to acknowledge that God did require
That the Jews form a clan, we can start to admire
That because they were faithful, our Saviour was born.
And we pray they'll all join us, the devil to scorn.

7 *God is Not in Control*

When people say that God is in control,
They do not understand the devil's role.
In Genesis the devil's scheme is laid.
He wants us to mistrust God's Word.
"Ye shall not surely die," was heard
By Eve who ate the fruit and disobeyed.

But Adam was the one who had to fall,
By choosing Eve and then forsaking all
That God had given him. He chose in haste.
Dominion and authority
Were handed over carelessly
To Satan. Adam threw the earth to waste.

Transference was thus legally received
By Satan who had subtly deceived.
The only way that God could change our plight,
For bound by His own rules He made,
His justice system He obeyed,
He sent His Son to earth to be our Light.

Take note that Adam's body did not die.
It almost seems that Satan did not lie.
But Adam's spirit did expire that day;
And so did his ability
To fellowship with God freely.
And to redeem us God did make a way.

Thus Jesus took on flesh to save us all,
To undo the transgression of the fall.
In Romans chapter five is Jesus named
The second Adam, righteousness,
To justify us through His death
Upon the cross and resurrection famed.

If you need further proof that this is true,
Then look in Matthew's gospel for a clue.
In chapter four does Satan try his best.
When Jesus fasted forty days,
And Satan tempted Him three ways,
But Satan failed when Jesus took his test.

In one temptation Satan took the Lord
Upon a mountain to show Him the world,
And claimed these kingdoms were all his to give.
Our Lord did not refute his claim.
He simply would not worship him.
His purpose was to die so we could live.

In chapter one of Job the seventh verse,
The Lord and Satan in this scene converse.
The devil tells the Lord from whence he came.
From earth was Satan, to and fro;
From earth, and not from hell below.
This plainly shows the earth is his domain.

To say that God is in control's a game
That is not wise; you're saying God's to blame.
But God is not the evil prince of earth.
So don't accuse of God bad things.
Confusion and mistrust this brings,
And means you do not understand your worth.

So if you want God's help, you must remember this key:
God's not in control unless you ask Him to be.
Ask Him as a group or individually.
But you must ask in Jesus' name.
He paid the price, us to redeem
To God. He's God's free gift to you and me.

8 *Pride*

Did you know it was pride that caused Satan to fall?
In Ezekiel, the twenty-eighth chapter tells all.
He was proud of his wisdom and beauty divine.
His desire to be greater than God warped his mind.

In Isaiah 14, verse thirteen and fourteen
Show how pride caused the devil to need to be seen.
This original sin from which evil began
Is a subtle, malignant obstruction to man.

It's acceptable when one is proud of the things
That are not the result of one's efforts to bring
Recognition to self. An example would be
When a Christian is proud that their Lord set them free.

But when pride causes one to be mindful of things
That are worldly and selfish, dishonor this brings.
Proverbs 29 verse twenty-three warns that pride
Will bring low your position. In shame you'll abide.

Yet in contrast we'll look at how Jesus did yield
His whole life to God's will, knowing His fate was sealed.
In Philippians 2, five to eight we can see
How our God became flesh so that we may be free.

In verse nine through eleven our Father He gave

His Son Jesus a name that's above every name.

When we emulate Jesus' example to love

Others better than self, we'll be blessed from above.

9 *The Serpent*

When the Israelites murmured against God's provision in the
Wilderness, in the twenty-first chapter of Numbers we see
In verse six that God sent fiery serpents among them and then
Many died who were bitten. And they did repent once again.

In verse seven they sought God's forgiveness through Moses, who
prayed.
The Lord told him to make a brass serpent and have it displayed
On a pole for all those who were bitten to look at and they
Would then live. This known symbol, caduceus, is still used today.

Now the serpent in Genesis 3 was more subtle than all
Other beasts of the field God had made. And as you may recall,
Evil Satan assumed this form when he tricked Adam and Eve.
Thus this creature was cursed and was cunningly used to deceive.

But this serpent, a symbol of Satan, became one of love.
For in John 3:14 the Lord tells us what would become of
His own self. Just like Moses did lift up the serpent, so He
Must be lifted up. Thus He became a curse so we'd be free.

Why did God not have Moses then use a real snake? We can see
This typology here of a snake points to Jesus, as He
Was a "likeness" of our sinful flesh when He died on the cross.
All God's judgment was poured out on Him and we gained from His
loss.

Now you'll notice God told them to look at the serpent to be
Saved from death. He did not want them looking at Moses, for he
Represented the Law. The Law's purpose was showing our need
For a Saviour, Lord Jesus. His death does fulfill it indeed.

10 *God's Protective Hedge*

If Satan hates us just as much as we
Learn in the Bible then to what degree
Are we protected from him causing grief?
If Satan could just kill us all,
He wouldn't wait for us to fall
Into his trap of sin and unbelief.

In Job we get a glimpse behind the mirror.
Behind the world we see and touch and hear.
Where God brags to the devil about Job.
There's none like him on earth you see.
He shuns all evil and fears Me.
But Satan's not impressed and wants to know

If Job would still fear God without reward.
The hedge of God's protection like a sword
To bless him in all that Job has and does.
Let Satan touch him, then we'll see.
If he is cursed will he still be
God's faithful servant like he always was?

Now Job is God's star player; he's God's best.
So God agrees to put him to the test.
Poor Job, he doesn't know he's in a game.
All hell is loosed on Job and clan,
More than it seems could any man
Survive, but still Job would not curse God's name.

That same hedge of protection we receive
When we ask God for it and we believe.
Don't fear a test like Job's; we're not that good.
But keep in mind that Satan cries
To God accusing us and tries
Our hedge to lower and us hurt he would.

Depending on the sin that we commit,
We certainly may have to pay for it.
But Satan must to God accuse us first.
The sins of pride and gossip can
Reduce the hedge of any man.
These two, plus unforgiveness are the worst.

But sometimes Satan doesn't even try
To hurt us; he's got bigger fish to fry.
The devil and his demons are the same
In number since the world began,
But population grows of man,
And Satan must be choosy who he'll frame.

So if one does not live for God and love
One's fellow man and share the gospel of
Our dear Lord Jesus, then one may be spared
From Satan's wrath and he may just
Decide there's nothing to mistrust.
Just leave them be. Why waste a demon there?

But if you love the Lord with all your heart
And want to spread the Gospel, just be smart.
And always be prepared for an attack.
When life gets hard and things go wrong,
Just trust the Lord. You must be strong.
Sufficient is God's grace; you do not lack.

11 *Three in One*

We are made up of three different parts. Three in one.
The most obvious member's our body, which runs
On the food that we eat; fuel that keeps us alive.
We are marvelous creatures, which God did contrive.

With our physical senses, all five that we name;
Sight and touch, taste and hearing and smell, we proclaim
What we like; what we don't. We experience all
That a life here on earth can afford, great and small.

Now our soul is the part that describes who we are.
It's our heart and our mind, and these words do by far
Interchange, for they represent how we all think
And behave. It's our person; what makes us distinct.

So what's left is our spirit; the portion that will
Live forever, as well as our soul. We will still
All be able to recognize who we once were.
Just our physical body returns to the earth.

Father God, He created us. He loves us more
Than we'll ever imagine; so much to be sure
That He gives us a choice. We must choose to believe
In His son, Jesus Christ. His free gift we receive.

This free gift is the chance for our spirits to dwell
In God's Heaven forever. If not then in hell
We will spend all eternity. Still it's a choice
We must make. Do we choose to regret or rejoice?

Now the wonderful thing that can happen if we
Accept Jesus, is His Holy Spirit, you see
Comes to live in our spirits. We do then become
Sons and daughters of God. Now we know where we're from.

But let's not get ahead of ourselves. We still do
Have this life here on earth to yet live and get through.
Understand that you don't have to do it alone.
If God lives in your spirit, you've help from the throne.

For your soul is the key. This is where you will make
All your choices in life. And you will make mistakes.
But if God lives in you, then in your mind He'll place
All good thoughts. He will guide you with love and His grace.

Be aware that the devil can still suggest wrong
Or bad thoughts. And your body will also have strong
Selfish wants and desires. But when you learn to "hear"
Thoughts from God, you'll be blessed. You'll have nothing to fear.

This is better than only depending on you;
Just your mind and your body to know what to do.
God the Father, the Son and the Spirit are three.
Three in One. We are made in His image you see.

12 *Contradictions*

Is it possible for there to be contradictions in the
Holy Bible? The answer is no, but some scriptures may be
Either misunderstood, or not translated properly. So
What translation can you put your trust in? King James. Good to
know.

Let us look at a verse that just doesn't make sense when compared
To most others. It's 1 John 3:9. This verse looks like a snare.
For it says, "Whosoever is born of God (saved, they do) not
Commit sin; for (God's) seed remains in (them)…" Be clear on this
thought.

For we all know we DO commit sin, even when we are saved.
It's impossible not to. Our flesh and minds can be depraved
When they're not governed by our saved spirit. That's where God
lives. We
Have His "seed," or His life, in our spirit. It's perfect you see.

And so what am I saying? Each one of us, we all have three
Distinct "parts." There's your body; the obvious one you can see.
And there's also your mind, which is known as your "heart," or
your "soul."
It's the part that your flesh and the world will attempt to control.

With our minds and our bodies, we do commit sin. But we don't,
Or "cannot" commit sin with our spirit, once saved. If you know
To do good, and don't do it, that's "sin," says James 4:17.
And so 1 John 3:9 now makes sense. Understand what it means.

For your mind, it's the KEY to your life here on earth. This is where
You make all your decisions; where choices are made. Be aware
That your spirit, where God lives, is perfect, but you must allow
It to govern your mind. Otherwise you won't change anyhow.

You can go on ignoring your spirit although you're saved. See,
God will not force His will on you. He gives you choice. You are free
To make your own decisions. God does not want robots. He'll wait
Very patiently for you to realize your life can be great.

Yes, your life can be wonderful when you allow your own mind
To be influenced by your saved spirit. God's peace you will find,
Passes all understanding. Let your mind be "kept" by the Lord,
As it says He will do in verse seven, Philippians 4.

13 *Intercession*

A most important lesson can be seen
From Jesus' parable in Luke 13.
In verses one through five where He replies
To stories of untimely deaths.
Did these men sin more than the rest?
And did this cause their premature demise?

"I tell you Nay," He answered to these few.
Lest ye repent the same will come to you.
What did He mean by this disturbing news?
Repent, it means to change one's mind,
Implying that their thoughts were blind
To truth. If they don't change their minds they'll lose.

In verses six through nine did He then tell
About a tree the owner wished to fell.
In three years it was fruitless; no figs grew.
The dresser of the vineyard dared
To ask if this tree could be spared
For one more year; he'd see what he could do.

The meaning of this parable is clear.
The dresser is the intercessor here.
He intervened to save the fig tree's fate.
And that is what we do when we
Give up our time to intercede
For others with our prayers. On God we wait.

So when you pray for others then you may
Prevent bad things from happening today.
And people who are blessed will never know
That they have you to thank for prayer,
Or that their very life was spared
Because you sacrificed your time to sow.

14 *Parable of the Sower*

The most crucial of parables for you to understand's one
That is taught in the Bible three times; all epistles but John.
To explain it, one could be compared to a garden that's sown
Full of seeds. Your crop hinges on soil where the seeds try to grow.

Do you tend to your garden? Do you make it fertile? Mark 4
Verse fourteen through verse twenty is where Jesus gives a secure
Explanation of three through verse eight. That's the parable. See
Verse eleven and twelve He explains some won't "get it." Indeed.

Verse thirteen is where Jesus explains this is crucial. If you
Do not understand this one, then none you'll discern. Sad but true.
Verse fourteen says the seed is the "word," word of God. There are
four
Types of "ground," (that's your mind) they will fall on. The outcome
is sure.

Verse fifteen is the ground by the way side; like ground 'round the
edge
Of one's garden. It's hard. It's not tilled. Seeds aren't likely to wedge
Themselves into the soil. That's when Satan comes promptly, you'll
find,
To take from you God's word so it doesn't get sown in your mind.

Verses sixteen and seventeen, this is the stony ground where
The word's heard and is gladly received, but no root takes place
there.

So when troubles arise for the word's sake, they cannot endure
Persecution or hardship. This Christian's a babe; not mature.

In verse eighteen and nineteen we see that the thorns are life's cares,
Wrong priorities, lusts, even guilt. These distractions, they snare
And they choke God's word. Even if these did believe for a while,
They now worry. Not focused on God. Not much reason to smile.

A consistent percentage, one fourth, are successful. They hear
And receive God's word. This is good ground. By respect God they
fear.
And they do bring forth fruit, as it says in verse twenty. Their minds
Are prepared to receive all God's promises. His peace they find.

So by now you can see that your garden's your heart, or your mind.
Are conditions within it prepared to receive God's divine
Words of life? Do you "till" it by spending some time in the Word?
Read your Bible, and pray, and be still, so His words can be "heard."

This key parable could be considered the Rosetta stone
Of the Bible's New Testament. This stone deciphered unknown
Heiroglyphics. So this advanced culture is now understood.
Well, this parable's like that. It leads you to insight that's good.

It explains why some "get it," and others do not. Even though
We're all given the same words of life, not that many will grow
In His grace. You can't bypass the root stage. Established you must
Be. God's word must take root in your life so His word you will trust.

15 *The Greatest Apostle*

Perhaps the greatest man who ever walked
This earth besides our dear Lord Jesus, talked
And still is talking to us in The Book.
Wrote most of the New Testament.
Once he met Jesus, his life spent
In furthering the Gospel; self-forsook.

A great man in the natural was Paul.
Philippians in chapter three tells all.
Verse five and six explain his pedigree.
A zealous Jew versed in the law,
A Pharisee without a flaw,
He persecuted Christians ruthlessly.

But back in chapter nine of Acts he met
The Lord Himself and never could forget
How wrong he'd been about the Lord and he
Endured the loss of everything,
And counted them but dung to bring
Himself to Christ for all eternity.

The first was Paul to understand and see
That once we're saved, Christ lives in us and we
Are crucified with Christ and dead to sin.
Galatians two and twenty names
Paul's revelation as he claims,
Through Christ we gain our righteousness and win.

16 *Clean Out Your Rain Spout*

Did you know that you have at the tip of your tongue a great prize
Not to be taken lightly. Ignoring this gift is not wise.
A prayer language of your very own's what you needed the most
When you asked the Lord Jesus to fill you with His Holy Ghost.

But the only way that you will know what potential you hold
To receive from this gift is to let your pride go and be bold.
You must take the first step to speak "words" that make no sense to you.
And show God by your act of submission that your heart is true.

It's the loss of control that's the issue for many, while some
Wait for their lips to move supernaturally, and play dumb.
This whole act is indeed supernatural, but it requires
Us to "act" out in faith and speak words that the Spirit inspires.

First Corinthians chapter 14 is where Paul does explain
About praying in tongues. In verse 2 this whole mystery's made plain.
When you pray in the Spirit, you're speaking to God; not to men.
And verse 4 says this edifies you. It is personal then.

So as Jesus does tell us in Matthew 6:6, we should pray
To our Father in secret, and He will reward us this way.
Romans 8:26 indicates that the Spirit does make
Intercession for us. Our infirmities are what's at stake.

By allowing the Spirit to send up to God prayers for you
That are not influenced by your own faulty thinking, He'll do
Some repairs to the flow of your rain spout; your mind that has been
Clogged by "leaves" and all kinds of life's "clutter" resulting from sin.

All the junk that's been clogging your rain spout includes all the woes
And wrong thinking that you've been exposed to. They impede the
flow
Of God's water that heals and brings life to your garden inside.
These include unforgiveness, religion and hatred and pride.

When the Spirit sends prayers up to God, then the answers return
Back to you in the form of His guidance through thoughts. You will
learn
That this "spiritual intuition's" more valuable to
You than all the world's riches. From this point it's all up to you.

As you learn to accept the Lord's guidance as help that you need,
You'll agree that He makes your life pleasant and helps you succeed.
As you grow in His grace, then the joy of the Lord will be yours.
He will lift heavy burdens. No longer will life be a chore.

But you should be aware that the devil does not like this prayer.
For he also does not know what "words" that you prayed, so don't
share
All the "answers" you get verbally. He will eavesdrop and try
To convince you these thoughts are no good. If you listen, he'll lie.

The most perfect example we have of what tongues can do for
Us is Paul the apostle who wrote about tongues, and much more.
Even Peter was stunned by Paul's wisdom that not even those
Same apostles who walked with our Lord for three years could
disclose.

First Corinthians 14:18's the assertion Paul made
Thanking God that he spoke in tongues more than the others. He
prayed
In the Spirit more than anyone had before, and was thus
The receiver of great revelations, and wrote them to us.

More than half the New Testament letters were written by Paul;
Making him the most influential Christian leader of all
The apostles. God spoke to his spirit and he did discern
That Christ lives in our spirits and guides us by grace. It's not earned.

Just remember, tongues edify you. In Jude 20 it's said
That you build up yourselves when you pray in the Spirit instead
Of just praying with your understanding. But as Paul relays;
You should pray with the Spirit as well as your mind every day.

17 *The Church Age of the Holy Ghost*

The Church of Jesus Christ began on Pentecost, when Jesus sent
The Holy Ghost to live among His followers. This great event
Is thus described in Acts the second chapter. After Peter gave
A bold discourse unto the crowd, three thousand more that day were
saved.

If we look back, remember Peter's weakness. He denied the Lord
Three times before the cock did crow, in fear, and then himself
abhorred
He for that lapse. But after Pentecost he gained the power of
The Holy Spirit. Dauntless he became, plus filled with Jesus' love.

Now this is just exactly what the Lord had planned. That's why He
gave
Us God the Holy Spirit as our Helper. All whom Jesus saves
Do gain the Holy Ghost within their spirits, and their spirits do
Then have the life of God in them. They're full of life. They've been
made new.

Accepting God's free gift of Jesus Christ is up to us. All we
Need do is recognize that Jesus is the Son of God, and He
Did take on flesh and live a human life like ours, but without sin.
Our sins he bore; became our Substitute. He died and rose again.

If you believe that this is true, then you're a child of God. And you
Now have the Holy Ghost. But don't stop there. You should continue to
Allow the Holy Spirit to renew your mind. You do this by
Thus using your prayer language which you now possess. Go on and try.

The first step you must take yourself. For some it bubbles up inside
Their mouths, but if you're like the rest, then apprehension set aside.
What helps is if you call God "Abba," for He is your Father, then
Repeat this word until the Holy Ghost controls your tongue. Amen.

This may seem foolish, but it's faith. Believe the Holy Spirit who
Now lives within your spirit is thus sending perfect prayers up to
Your Father. And the answers will return, although you do not know
What prayers were sent, but guaranteed the answers will then help you grow.

"What answers?" you may ask. "And what prayers did I make?" Well here's the thing.
This practice of God's presence is most flawless, for you do not bring
The errors of your thinking into the equation. Leave them out.
Just trust the Holy Spirit, for He knows your needs, so have no doubt.

And down the road, just when you least expect it, suddenly you will
Know what to do when faced with situations you before were ill
Prepared to deal with. This is just a broad example of what He
Provides. Who wouldn't want God's help to live their lives? Don't you agree?

But most importantly, the Holy Spirit will equip us to
Help spread the Gospel, for the great commission is for us to do
The works that Jesus did, but greater. We should let all others know
The wonders of His love and gift of life, and also help them grow.

Let's look at the Apostle Paul. The Lord he met in chapter 9
Of Acts. He had the greatest revelations of them all. And time
He spent, yes years, himself preparing for what he must do for the
Lord. Paul did pray in tongues more than the rest which lead to his
esteem.

In Second Timothy and chapter 3 verse one through five we see
What life on earth will thus be like the closer that we get to the
Return of Christ. The end of the Church Age is when Lord Jesus, He
Comes back. This time is now upon us. See how true these verses be.

Verse five says some will have a form of godliness, but still deny
The power thereof. This means that they do not believe, or even try
To understand that once they're saved, they have the Holy Ghost
and He
Does give them power within themselves to live their lives with
majesty.

With majesty? Yes we are all the "righteousness" of Jesus Christ.
We're not supposed to make our plans without Him and throw darts
at life.
And notice at the end of this verse, five, it says to "turn away
From *such*," from those who don't believe the Holy Ghost gives
power today.

18 *Vertical*

Your relationship with Father God, it is vertical. Think
"Up and down." Your behavior does not change His love for you.
Drink
Of His life giving water. His Spirit lives in you. He deals
With you Spirit to spirit. Don't focus on just how you feel.

For we all have those days that are bad. And yes, even on your
Very worst day He loves you, not more or not less than before.
From the moment that Jesus was born did the angels proclaim
In Luke 2 God's good will "toward" men. Things were never the
same.

Oh yes, God was at war with mankind in Old Testament days.
But in Second Corinthians 5 verse nineteen it does say,
 "To wit, God was in Christ, reconciling the world to himself,
Not imputing their trespasses…" So with our sins He has dealt.

Horizontal is how you affect those around you, and that
Is where sin can be hurtful, like gossip or stealing. If at
Any time you feel guilty and worry God's mad at you; don't.
If you think God will punish you for what you did; no He won't.

But the problem with sin is you're playing with fire. You'll get burned.
And don't blame it on God. He's not punishing you. Instead learn
That you opened the door to the world. That's the devil's domain.
When you're bad horizontally, then only you can you blame.

It's the goodness of God that will lead to repentance. Verse four,
Romans 2. For God gave us His Son. He's not mad anymore.
When you know that you're righteous, and how much He loves you,
then you
Will repent (change your mind) and His goodness you'll demonstrate
too.

19 *Three Sources*

Did you know you are made in God's image? That's why you have three
Distinct parts, just like God is three parts of a whole Trinity.
There's your flesh. It's the natural part that is easy to see
And to feel. There's your spirit that will for eternity "be."

Now the part that's important's your *SOUL*. This is where you receive
All your guidance in life. It's your mind; where you think and believe.
It's where spiritual warfare takes place. So now let us discuss
The three sources from which you get guidance. In whom do you trust?

If your trust is in God, then you're ten steps ahead of the crowd.
Through your spirit He guides you, as much as your soul has allowed
You to hope. If you're open to His thoughts, His nature, how He
Sees things, you will be one who He leads supernaturally.

Now the "Zoe" of God is the "stuff" that His Spirit is made
Of; the *LIFE* that went into your spirit the moment you prayed
To the Lord and He saved you. His life is the "light" that's inside
You. And now you're a light in the world. Let it shine. Do not hide.

There are two other sources that influence you and your mind,
Or your soul. The most logical one is yourself. You will find

That your flesh can be selfish. It wants what it wants. So you learn
To control it. Your brain's the important part. That's your concern.

If you're stubborn and see things as you think they should be then
you
May be quenching the fruits of the spirit that made you a new
Creature. They include love, joy and peace and longsuffering. These
Can be found in Galatians 5:22 and 23.

In Ephesians 4:17 we are thus urged not to be
Like the ones in 4:18 who walk in the blind vanity
Of their minds. Their discernment is darkened. They cannot perceive
That they're alienated from God for they do not believe.

In Galatians and 5:17 Paul informs us we're in
A perpetual battle of flesh against spirit. To sin
Is the natural tendency flesh follows, contrary to
What the fruits of the spirit, now in you, will guide you to do.

There is one more source, evil; that's Satan. His only attack
Against children of God is through broadcasting thoughts. And he
lacks
The ability God has to read your mind. All he can do
Is observe your reaction to thoughts he imposed upon you.

Just say "No." That is the best defense against Satan. Ignore
Him and he'll go away in due time. But if you are "weak," your
Best protection's Philippians 4 and verse eight, for it tells
You to "think on these things" that are good. This will guard your
mind well.

When you learn to receive from your Spirit, where God lives, then He

Is enabled to guide you through life. You'll be able to "see"

Things you couldn't before, and your life will be joyful. His will

For your life, you will also want. You will be blessed and fulfilled.

20 *Practicing His Presence*

This poem is based on the account given by Frank Laubach
in the book "Practicing His Presence."

In "Practicing His Presence" there's a missionary, Laubach, who
Does give account of his experiment in 1930. Through
His loneliness when serving on an island in the Philippines,
Completely he surrendered his own mind and will to God it seems.

'Tis wonderful that he did keep a journal to record each day
Results of his endeavor to stay focused on the Lord this way.
At first his mind did wander and he'd know that gaps of time had
passed
Where he did think of other things. Could he improve? Himself he
asked.

When Mr. Laubach learned to nurture fellowship with God, and he
"Let go" of things that made God vanish from his mind, then he did
see
This eager attitude towards God did have rewards, and all the more
Determined he became to let God melt his heart right to its core.

The interesting thing he found was though this concentration to
Stay focused every minute on the Lord was strenuous, a new
Discovery he made was that all else he did in life was now
Not strenuous at all. His daily chores were effortless somehow.

He thought more clearly, less forgot, and things that were a strain before
He now did easily and without effort. Worried he no more.
He lost no sleep. He walked on air. And even in the mirror strong
Did light shine in his face. When God was there then nothing could go wrong.

Began he to see people with a love God gave, and noticed they
This love, as if they were compelled to follow him. Is this the way
That Jesus drew the crowds to Him? His "God-intoxicated" grace
Of endless fellowship with God did lure to Him the human race.

He then returned to busy life and he determined he must take
The Lord with him into the crowds, and still continue thus to make
His conversations with the Lord. This silent heart to heart discourse
Allowed him interaction with the world while making God his source.

As he did grow and learn to love this way of life that he did find
By accident, he understood that he must share this peace of mind
Afforded him by God Himself. He then began to think of ways
To teach to others what he learned. So read about his glorious days.

His best advice is to become God's friend, just like a child would grow
In closeness with their parent. But a friendship must be nurtured so
It does not stagnate. Friendships are progressive, so devote your time
To Him. Abide in His love and allow Him to renew your mind.

The same results can be achieved by praying in the spirit as
This practice of God's presence. Both require an act of will and have
A need for concentration and devotion of your time, but this
Becomes a habit and gets easy. Your reward from God is bliss.

21 *The Seventieth Week*

A great statement is made unto Abraham, Father of Jews.
God Himself says in Genesis 12 the third verse what He'll do.
Now our God is eternal and time does not change what He says.
If He said it, He meant it. This promise is meant for all days.

So take heed that the Jews are God's people He blessed with His word.
And through them did He bless all the families of earth with our Lord.
Though some Jews still have yet to accept their Messiah was here.
God's word speaks, "treat the Jews with respect," and His word we should fear.

In the Bible God's plans are revealed if we read them with care.
God's beloved prophet Daniel's great prophecy with us he shared.
Daniel 9 verses twenty-four through twenty-seven explain
Of the seventieth week God has planned for the Jews who remain.

Now this prophecy has not fulfilled. It continues today.
For the seventieth week will occur at a time God won't say.
Tribulation is when this said "week," but in years will take place.
And these last seven years are the last chance one's sins to erase.

Thus seventy weeks are determined upon all the Jews.
By a "week" is meant years, so four hundred and ninety is used.
And in verse twenty-five it accounts for the first sixty-nine.
The first seven are separate (times seven is forty and nine).

It took forty-six years as recorded in John chapter two
To rebuild the temple as ordered by Cyrus to do.
Most agree that the extra three years were to find builders skilled
In the arts and to gather and transport materials to build.

This leaves sixty-two weeks then until the Messiah's demise.
"But not for himself," is the way we know Jesus did die.
So from four-fifty-four, plus the forty-nine years brings us to
B.C. four-o-five, then add four hundred thirty-four too.

Amazingly we're at A.D. twenty-nine which is when
Our Lord Jesus, He died to bring life and His peace to all men.
Thus we live in this age in between before Jesus returns.
God has never forgotten the Jews; their importance we'll learn.

In verse twenty-six is the antichrist mentioned, and then
Twenty-seven reveals tribulation's midpoint which is when
The seventieth week shall occur. There'll be one who steps out
With solutions. And this is the antichrist cautioned about.

Tribulation is taught only sixty-four times in The Book.
So it must be important to God. In a gospel we'll look.
Matthew's gospel the twenty-fourth chapter is where Jesus taught
Of the seventieth week which is for all the Jews who are caught

In the end of this age. Matthew twenty-four from verse thirteen
To verse thirty forewarns of the end. Verse thirteen is between,
Or the midpoint of the tribulation. And "saved" in this verse
Does not mean "born again," but instead, that endured ye the worst.

Verse sixteen it refers to the Jews… "Then let them which be
In Judea flee into the mountains." God tells them to flee.
And also they're warned against prophets who'd have them believe
In false Christs. But the end has not come yet so be not deceived.

Tribulation then ends and verse thirty says Jesus appears.
There'll be mourning because it's too late at this point to have tears.
When He comes in His glory, no doubt there will be that He's King.
Rejecting God's Christ thus the ultimate penalty brings.

Daniel 9 twenty-six, it was written before the command
Long before Christ was born to rebuild the Lord's temple by hand.
Yet this verse tells exactly when Jesus would die, which attests
If you trust in God's word, and your life trust in Him, you'll be
blessed.

22 *Nicodemus*

In Jesus' time the Pharisees were the
Religious leaders, privileged as can be.
A learned group who knew God's law complete.
And Nicodemus was of the elite.

But just like any system run by man,
Corrupt they got and lost their power to stand
Against the devil. Hypocrites they were.
Their blessings lost. Their God they could not stir.

In John 3:1 to 21 we see
A poignant tale where Nicodemus, he
Did come by night to Jesus to inquire
If He's from God. To know he did desire.

Then Jesus, He perceived that this man be
Dissatisfied with his theology.
A spiritual testament He gave
To Nicodemus. He showed him the way.

Again in chapter 7 near the end,
Verse 50 and verse 51 defends
He Jesus from his very own who seek
To take His life. No longer is he weak.

The last we read in John about this man
In chapter 19:39 we can
Observe that he in Jesus now believes.
He helped with Jesus' body to retrieve.

The mark that Jesus made upon his heart
With words of wisdom so profound did start
His mind to want more than mere men could give.
So he chose life and now his spirit lives.

23 *The Lost are Found*

The parables that Jesus told were such
That they bewildered lawful Jews so much.
The Pharisees were always close at hand
Near Jesus. What He taught they could not stand.

In Luke 16, verse fifteen and sixteen
Does Jesus tell the Pharisees they'd seen
The last that would be preached of Moses' Law.
This antiquated Covenant had flaws.

The time had come for a New Covenant.
The Heavens would rejoice that God had sent
His Dear Son Jesus to set all men free
From bondage to serve laws they could not keep.

Thus from the time that Adam sinned and fell,
'Til Jesus died and took our sins to hell,
The world was lost. Galatians chapter 3
And 4 explain how Jesus set us free.

In Luke 15 there is a story told
By Jesus. The New Covenant unfolds
In this great parable. We now can see
That when we're saved, it's individually.

To God are we, thus each and every one,
Important as the next. His work is done.
When found is just one son, one coin, one sheep,
The Heavens do rejoice that life we reap.

The story of the prodigal son's ease
Must greatly have displeased the Pharisees.
Forgiveness was a trait not to be found
In Moses' Law. By rules the Jews were bound.

For in the Law, in Deuteronomy,
This reckless son would have been stoned, to be
A grave example to all those who would
Consider doing not but what they should.

This jealous brother in verse twenty-eight
To thirty does exemplify the hate
That the Old Covenant could not conceal.
So Lord, we thank you that your Love is real.

Thus this New Covenant that Jesus brings
Will bless your life and make you want to sing
His praises. For forgiveness is just one
Of many blessings that we all have won.

24 *God Paints a Picture*

God our Father, He paints a clear picture of Jesus throughout
The Old Testament, all but in Proverbs. There should be no doubt.
There are clues of His coming. The first is in Genesis 3.
God warns Satan that born of a woman his rival would be.

Then there's Joseph, who was just like Jesus in so many ways.
The Lord blessed him in all that he touched, and his brothers forgave
He for selling him into captivity. Also he took
Him a bride of the gentiles, like Jesus, whose own Him forsook.

Though the Israelites murmured repeatedly after God freed
Them from bondage in Egypt, He kindly supplied all their needs.
They complained that the waters at Marah were bitter, and then
Moses threw in a tree and the water became sweet again.

Once again then the picture of Jesus is painted, for He
Did His life sacrifice for us all on a cross, or a "tree."
Bread from heaven, or manna, did fall, just like Jesus who's the
Bread from heaven that's "true," as He says in John 6:33.

Once did Moses the Law bring the Israelites, and they did fail
To obey God's commandments, their sin then against them prevailed.
Our High Priest, Jesus Christ, is described in Leviticus. He
Poured His blood in the Holy of Holies in Heaven you see.

The man-made Tabernacle on earth is a likeness of the
Tabernacle in Heaven, and yearly the high priest was he
Who was able to enter God's dwelling on earth. But the Lord,
He died once. With his blood we're made righteous. To God we're
restored.

In Isaiah the fifty-third chapter, His death is described
Better than anyone who did witness first hand His demise.
Several hundreds of years was this prophecy made before He,
Jesus Christ gave Himself to the world so that we could be free.

Now consider what happened when His two disciples were on
A long walk to Emmaus, and talked of how Jesus was gone,
In the 24th chapter of Luke. Jesus joined them and they
Didn't know it was Him who explained why He'd died on that day.

And beginning at Moses, throughout the Old Testament, He
Showed them all of the scriptures that pointed to Him, so they'd see
Without knowing Him plainly, the Bible is all about Him.
So we too can see how the Old points to the New, just like them.

25 *Jesus is the Word*

Our Lord Jesus is just as much God as our Father Above.
He was known as the "Word" long before He revealed His great love
By becoming a man and forever forfeiting His place
Of equality with God the Father, to save our whole race.

After Satan deceived God's creation in Genesis three,
In the fifteenth verse God did warn Satan his rival would be
A man born of the seed of the woman, and that this man would
Bruise his head, which is vital, so fight this he would if he could.

For a blow to the head meant defeat, just as surely as death.
It'd be better to keep his opponent from taking one breath.
But the seed of the woman was not very narrow a clue.
So the battle began and Messiah the devil pursued.

But in Genesis twenty-two verse seventeen and eighteen
God told Abraham that He would bless all the earth through his seed.
Thus Messiah would come from this family, one could attest.
Then God further, in forty-nine ten, declared Judah be blessed.

Then Isaiah sixteen and verse five did prophetically tell,
From King David's descendants Messiah would be born as well.
From the time that the Lord manifested, the devil did try
To destroy Him. But God had appointed the time He would die.

When the time for Lord Jesus to suffer drew near He did pray
To His Father in Heaven. In John seventeen He does say
That all those who believe He is Lord will be one with both He
And His Father. He's not of this world and thus neither are we.

If the devil had any idea how His death would go down.
That by shedding His blood for us all would earn Jesus the crown.
The three days that He spent down below with the weight of all sins,
Without sin of His own, justified us. Our pardon He wins.

So the devil unknowingly helped carry out his defeat.
Romans five verses eight through eleven show Christ did complete
Our atonement. No longer can Satan impose on us death.
Christ brings life to our spirits and justified are we by faith.

26 *Communion*

Jesus taught us to look on His body and blood for our health.
It's a ploy of the devil to get you to focus on "self."
Never once did He mention your sins that you need to confess.
How we see the Lord's body is all that we need to address.

First Corinthians chapter eleven, verse twenty-three through
To verse thirty reflect the Communion which Jesus did do
On the night He was by his disciple named Judas betrayed,
For to "shew the Lord's death till He come," was this offering made.

When He told us these elements take, "in remembrance of Me,"
He wants all to remember His death on the cross, us to free.
When we do this in honor of Him, then the bread and the poured
Are in fact transformed into the body and blood of the Lord.

When Paul said to "examine yourself" before you eat and drink,
This has been misconstrued by the devil who wants you to think
Of yourself and your sins; how unworthy are you. What a worm.
This is Not about you or your sins. With the devil be firm.

You are only to think on Lord Jesus and His sacrifice.
The Lord died for your sins and your sicknesses. He paid the price.
The whole point of examining self is to make sure you see
That the bread and the cup show how much He loves both you
and me.

Thus the benefit of this Communion is widely ignored.

This is God's own prescription for health and well-being restored.

If you take it "unworthily," all that you get is a snack.

If we focus on Him, then His goodness we all will not lack.

27 *The Passover Lamb*

Jesus fits the description in Exodus 12 to a tee
Of a Passover lamb, for our Passover Lamb thus is He.
First Corinthians five and verse seven does give Him this name.
The Old Testament scriptures do show us why Paul made this claim.

In Exodus 12 and verse two it describes this event
As the first, or beginning of months. It does show God's intent
Was for them to bethink "New Beginning." A new day has dawned.
The beginning of trusting in God for deliverance spawned.

And for our new beginning we must recognize that our Lord
Jesus Christ is our Passover Lamb. Thus we cannot afford
Not to see that His death on the cross was a once and done deal.
Our atonement is paid with His blood. Our redemption is real.

When comparing then Exodus 12 to Luke 20 we see
That five days Jesus entered Jerusalem so He could be
Thus examined before the Jews' Passover, so He could show
That He was without blemish. His purpose the Jews did not know.

For in Exodus 12 and verse three through verse six they were bid
To examine this lamb from the tenth to the fourteenth to rid
Any doubt that no blemish it had. For five days it was thus
Under scrutiny, just like our Lord was inspected for us.

First examined was He by the leaders religious who sought
To know by what authority did He these things, for He taught
In the temple. Luke 20 verse three through verse eight, His reply
Gave them no chance to stump Him. No fault could they find when
they tried.

In Luke 20, verse twenty-one through twenty-six shows how He
Did the next exam pass. With the wisdom of God He decrees
We should render to Caesar the things that are Caesar's, and we
Should thus render to God what is His. Words to live by are these.

Thus obey all the laws of the land where you live, just as long
As they don't contradict what's important to God. It is wrong
For example to snuff out the life of an unwanted youth.
This is outlined in Romans 13; we must first seek God's truth.

Then in verse twenty-seven through thirty-three Jesus was asked
By the Sadducees a pointed question. His answer was that
They knew nothing of what they were asking. In verse thirty-four
On to verse thirty-eight, He states we would be married no more.

Then in Luke 23, after Jesus was captured, they brought
Him to Pilate, who sent Him to Herod. These men found no fault
In our Lord. But the chief priests and scribes did Him fiercely accuse
Of perverting the nation and claiming to be King of Jews.

So this innocent man, our Redeemer from God, did fulfill
What is stated in Exodus 12 and verse six, that they kill
Then their Passover Lamb in the evening, in the assembly
Of the Israelites. Picture Him on the cross at Calvary.

Then in Exodus 12 verse eleven, instructed were they
To be clothed and be ready, and eat their Passover this way.
Expectation and joy was their attitude purposed to be.
This is verified also in Psalms 105:43.

And in Psalms 105:37 it shows that they all
Were brought forth out of Egypt with money and health. Thus our call
As God's children continues to be "healthy, wealthy and glad."
And our Passover Lamb does not want us to lack or be sad.

What's your attitude then? Do you think Jesus cares about things
That you face every day? Yes He does. And belief in Him brings
All that's good. Do you see Him as your New Beginning? Then you
Are now well on your way to a life that's exciting and new.

28 *Isaiah 53*

When we regard Isaiah 53,
We think about the cross on Calvary,
Where Jesus paid the price; our Substitute.
On Him all sins of man did God impute.

But so much more He did for us that day.
He also bore our sicknesses away.
Redemption does include your healing too.
So it's available to me and you.

Isaiah 53 verse 4 is one
Where accurate translation was not done.
It says our "griefs" and "sorrows" He did bare.
We'll check the Greek translation if we dare.

The word translated "grief" is "makob" here.
In Job this word means "pain," so was there fear?
And seven other times is "choli" used
As "sickness," yet here "sorrows" was misused.

No matter if translations these were wrong.
In Matthew 8 and 17 is strong
Clear evidence that "sicknesses" were meant.
Isaiah to fulfill was Jesus sent.

In the New Testament the strongest text
There is for healing we will go to next.
John 14:12 and 13 Jesus claims
We'll get what we ask for in Jesus' name.

In other words the Holy Spirit He
Had in His spirit working, so do we.
And thus we will do even greater things.
Authority we have that His name brings.

In Proverbs chapter 4 is wisdom found.
Verse 20 through to 22 is sound
Strong wisdom from God's word; in your heart keep.
And health to all your flesh and life you'll reap.

29 *The Body and the Blood*

The church of Jesus Christ began on Pentecost, when Jesus sent
The Holy Ghost to live among His followers. This great event
Is thus described in Acts the second chapter. After Peter gave
A bold discourse unto the crowd, three thousand more that day were
saved.

Remained they in Jerusalem where they did fellowship and live
In commune, as described in verses forty-two through forty-six.
And daily they were breaking bread from house to house,
remembering
The sacrifice their Lord had made for them. His praises they did sing.

And so began this practice of communion, as described by Paul
In the eleventh chapter of Corinthians the First, when all
Disciples of the Lord partook of bread and wine He gave to them.
"This is my body...and my blood," He told them, to remember Him.

These elements, they represent the "body" and the "blood" of He
Who gave His life for us, and we do honor Him when we believe.
The very life of Christ comes in our bodies when we do consume
The bread and wine. Where God is, sickness cannot stay. There is no
room.

So understand, the "Zoe" or the "stuff" that makes God "God" is in
Your body now. No sickness can survive, and you are free of sin.
So why not do this every day, at home? The wine you can replace
With grape juice if you want. Christ gave His life to save the human
race.

The Lord Himself did tell us in John 6, verse fifty-three and to
Verse fifty-eight, unless you eat His flesh and drink His blood, then
you
Have no life in you. But the only way that's possible for one
To do this is believe the bread and wine do represent God's Son.

The Lord's apostles never asked for healing for themselves, for they
Did have communion, God's prescription for their health. Though
they did pray
For others. But before the Lord ascended, the Passover gave
A yearly only chance for health, and means for all their sins to waive.

In Exodus and chapter twelve the Israelites did first partake
Of the Passover lamb. In verses eight and nine they were to make
Sure it was roasted. They were not to eat it raw. This would compare
To Jesus then before the cross, who all our sins and ills did bear.

And also they were told the lamb not sodden down with water eat.
In other words, don't water down the gospel. Do not make it weak.
It's not about confessing sins. It's not just for forgiveness. The
Whole purpose of communion's for our body, soul and mind to free.

30 *The Bread of Life*

In the Old Testament, From Exodus to Deuteronomy,
The Israelites were in the wilderness, though Moses brought them free
From Egypt. They did murmur against God and so they lost their right
To occupy the Promised Land. They did not walk by faith, but sight.

For many were the miracles that God performed to bring them out
Of Egypt. After parting the Red Sea, there should have been no doubt
That God would do exactly what He said. In Numbers 21,
Verse five complained they once again, despite the battle they'd just won.

The manna that sustained them forty years, they loathed, and they did call
"Light bread," which in the Hebrew means it's "worthless." Grateful? Not at all.
And in verse six the Lord sent fiery serpents. Many died and they
Then came to Moses seeking God's forgiveness; asking him to pray.

Verse eight and nine describe the Lord's solution. He bid Moses make
A fiery serpent which he set upon a pole, for those to take
A look at who'd been bitten, and they would not die. This previews the
Lord Jesus who was lifted on a cross for all the world to "see."

In Numbers 21 did Moses thus explain the reason for
Lord Jesus' death upon the cross. In John 3:14 says the Lord
That just as Moses lifted up the serpent in the wilderness,
Must He be lifted up as well, to save us all from spiritual death.

In the New Testament, John chapter six is powerful indeed,
Containing the Lord's testimony that He's the "true bread," we read.
And just like manna, He came down from heaven. But the difference
is
That all who eat the Bread of Life, Himself, will thus forever live.

In verses fifty-three through fifty-eight He gives a picture of
The purpose of communion. He did die for us to show His love.
Except ye eat His flesh and drink His blood, you have no life in you.
Who wouldn't want His life in them? Let's honor Him in all we do.

31 *You Cannot Lose Your Salvation*

Every now and then you'll hear it preached
That your salvation can be lost, or breached.
This simply is not true. Once you get saved,
You're saved, no matter how you misbehave.

One verse contributing to this mistake
Is Romans 8 verse six from which some take
One's loss to be from carnal mindedness.
But this does not mean "spiritual death."

If this were true, we'd all be "dead" because
How can you make your mind behave? It does
Not take but a few seconds and your mind
Is on some great diversion, you will find.

It means "death" to the operation of
The Spirit, such as peace and joy and love.
Galatians 5, verse twenty-two and three
Names all the Spirit's fruits for you and me.

But carnal mindedness is not at all
Times evil. It just means you're thinking small.
You're thinking worldly thoughts; things not of God.
And on your thoughts the Spirit will not trod.

Now once the Holy Spirit lives in you,
He will make you feel guilty if you do
Not do what's right. But you can quench Him by
Repeatedly refusing to comply.

So how can one control one's every thought?
This takes a lot of practice to be taught
To train one's mind to think on spiritual things.
But peace and life and happiness this brings.

Philippians 4:8, it does express
How to achieve spiritual mindedness.
So if you want God's peace, "think on these things."
For peace and life and happiness this brings.

Ephesians 4, verse thirty tells us not
To grieve the Holy Spirit, Who you got
When you got saved, and whereby you are sealed
Until the day that Christ returns revealed.

32 *Demonic Hindrance*

Once we understand God is a Spirit, and that's how He deals
With His children, us, Spirit to spirit, this knowledge reveals
Revelation important to us. For 1 John 3 verse eight
And verse nine could confuse one not knowing this circumstance
great.

For it says in these verses, if we commit sin we are not
Born of God, but the devil. Upsetting is this. Although what
This does not thus explain is God lives in our spirit, and so
With our spirit no sin can we do. This is good then to know.

Do we sin with our flesh and our soul (or our mind)? Yes we do.
This is why once we're saved it's important our minds to renew.
When we do sin it does not affect our relationship we
Have with God, for His seed's in our spirit for eternity.

This earth body we have is what gives us authority to
Deal with demons and Satan himself. They oppress all that do
Not know how to avoid or rebuke them. And some let them in
To their lives and they don't even know they're indulging in sin.

This demonic oppression or hindrance, it can hinder you
From receiving from God. So remember, they're limited to
Only broadcasting thoughts, which they'll try to get you to accept.
If they can they'll manipulate you. In their grip you'll be kept.

They will tell you you're sick, and then you'll feel the symptoms. And you
Will then reap the results of your thoughts. So what then can you do?
Well unless you are strong and do stand on God's promise, you're ill.
But remember, for you to be sick, this is never God's will.

There are "faults" you can have, and they may have been dumped on you by
Evil demons who prompt you to have selfish thoughts. They will try
To arouse you to sin. Unforgiveness is one that is bad.
Also anger or pride, or worse, gossip. They're hurtful and sad.

All these things allow Satan to have some control over you.
And the one you hurt most is yourself, plus what Satan may do
When your hedge of protection from God is thus lowered. Don't be
So naïve to think you will not pay when you act selfishly.

So take caution of what you permit to go into your mind.
Chapter 4 and verse eight of Philippians, that's where you'll find
All the thoughts that will keep you above and not let you sink down
To the level where thoughts from the devil will cause you to frown.

There's one other infallible way to defend one's own soul,
And that's praying in tongues, for renewing your mind is the goal.
Read Acts 2, the new church, they received their new tongues on the day
That they first did believe and got the Holy Ghost right away.

The "church age" we are in, it began then in Acts chapter 2.
These first Christians behaved as we should; like they had been made
"new."
If we recognize that God is with us, and greater is He
That's in us than he that's in the world, then empowered are we.

This is spiritual warfare. Ephesians 6:12 does define
That the battle is not physical. It is all in your mind.
And so once we're aware of this battle, we can do our part.
For these demons go after our leaders. That's where they will start.

It is easy to see that world leaders are influenced by
Evil demons. Just look at the mess in the world. This is why
When we pray in the spirit, our prayers are not limited to
What we know. God can use our prayers to do what He needs to do.

33 *Spiritual Warfare*

There is a world that's just beyond the reach
Of our five senses physical which teach
Us how to deal with all things natural.
The world we sense through what is tangible.

But faith, it gives us the ability
To trust that there's a world we cannot see.
It's all around us. We are just the pawns
Set on this worldly stage that we live on.

There is a battle that is taking place,
Manipulating all the human race.
The Lord, He has equipped us for this fray.
Important is our readiness to pray.

Ephesians 6, verse twelve tells of this war.
The devil is the one who's keeping score.
This war is real. It's happening today.
Just watch the news. You'll see it plain as day.

This verse, it warns of spiritual beings
Of wickedness who lurk behind the scenes.
The evil prince of earth and all his band
Of demons, with the devil, rule our land.

Ephesians 6, read past verse twelve and through
Eighteen. These verses tell us what to do

To gird ourselves for spiritual war.
And this is where we even out the score.

Ephesians 1, eighteen until the end,
And chapter 2, verse one and six defend
That we are seated with the Lord on the
Right hand of God the Father, spiritually.

Thus we are elevated to a place
Above the enemy that we do face.
How do we battle what we cannot see?
With humble prayer that's offered earnestly.

We pray, and angels of protection are
Thus loosed to fight for goodness in this war.
We pray, and evil demons become bound
On earth, to be cast out upon the ground.

We wrestle not against the flesh and blood.
For people aren't the problem, so we should
Be wary of the spirit that's behind
Them, cultivating evil in their minds.

And so you see, it's up to us to pray.
To fight the fight of faith, as some would say.
We are the church, or body of the Lord.
He is a Spirit. We must wield the sword.

34 *Evil Corrupts Good*

Why is it, do you think, that when a person who is good
Surrounds himself or herself with some folks they know they should
Not "hang" with, thinking that their righteousness will influence
The others, this is not the case. They're straddling the fence.

For easier it is to fall than what it is to get
Back up. Let's face it; sin is fun, but costly. So just let
God deal with sinners His way, in His time. But otherwise
Seek first the things above; eternal. Do not compromise.

And know that when God "nudges" you to speak to someone's heart
About Him, He will make it easy for you. Do your part
By living as it says in Titus 2:11 and
2:12. Let Jesus' grace affect your life and be His friend.

The Bible gives examples of how evil can pervert
Someone that's good, just like a little leaven does convert
The lump. Corinthians the First 5:6 to 13's where
Paul warns to wisely choose your friends; to leaven sin's compared.

King Solomon was blessed beyond belief by God, but he
Loved many women strange, although God's warning was to flee
From such. He did not listen and his heart was turned away
From God; as in 11:2 of First Kings it does say.

And as it says in Titus 2:14, the Lord Himself
He gave, redeeming us from evil. Do not let your self
Be influenced by any other. Purified are we
Through Him. "Peculiar people," that is what we strive to be.

35 *Peace and Rest*

Good tidings of great joy were brought to earth that glorious day
When Jesus, God's own Son, became a man to pave the way
For all mankind. Redeemed us He to Father God above.
For God our Father wants us all to know that He is Love.

Luke 2 verse eight to fourteen speaks the angel of the Lord
To shepherds keeping watch. The host of heaven states "toward"
All men good will from God, and peace on earth. But notice they
Did not say peace "among" all men; for this is not God's way.

The earth is still a mess and so does evil still abound.
The devil never went away; he's very much around
Deceiving man. But God has given all of us a choice.
Receive His dear Son Jesus by believing, and rejoice.

In Matthew 10 verse thirty-four does Jesus say that He
Came not to send the world His peace. But in our minds do we
Receive this blessing when the Holy Ghost does permeate
Our thinking, when we choose to dwell on things not small, but great.

Philippians 4:8 does tell us how to think on things
Not fleeting of this earth, but broadening our thinking brings
Us peace. So let your troubles go and let your spirit soar.
First Peter 5 verse seven does remind of this and more.

Philippians 4:7 does describe the peace that He
Awards us. In Luke 12 verse thirty-four to fifty-three
Explains the Lord, there is a cost to living selfishly.
'Tis better to prepare one's heart for Him, for blessed we'll be.

One does not need to be absorbed with personal desires
And needs. Luke 12 verse twenty-nine through thirty-one inspires
Us to put God our Father first, for He knows what we need.
He wants us all, His children to be happy and succeed.

Thus "peace" and "rest" they do go hand in hand, by now you see.
So enter into Father's rest and let your mind be free
Of burdens. Matthew quotes our Lord in verses twenty-eight
To thirty of eleven: take His yoke; He'll lift your weights.

So when you give your life to Jesus, where will you then be?
You'll still be you, but better, and the truth you now will see.
And though the world is troubled all around, you've been released
From fear and other weights. His Spirit fills your mind with peace.

36 *Free From the Law*

In the beginning, the sins of all men were not charged.
Unencumbered by laws, the whole race of God's children enlarged
One vast circle of evil. And free to chaotically choose
To do all that they willed without harm; there was nothing to lose.

The first murder, when Cain did kill Abel, there was no real cost
For this sin. And God's mercy extended to all who were lost
Just like Cain. But eventually God did destroy nearly all
Of creation. Instructed He Noah who answered God's call.

And a covenant was thus established in Genesis 9
And verse eight to eleven. The rainbow forever a sign
That no longer would God destroy with a great flood all the earth.
Set in motion God's plan of redemption which lead to Christ's birth.

God began His design with the faithful man Abraham who
In God's promise believed; that all nations would him be blessed
through.
Thus accounted for righteousness was his belief, and it states
In Galatians 3:6 to 3:9, blessed are all who have faith.

From four thousand B.C. 'til about fifteen hundred B.C.
Was no knowledge of sin, and God's mercy was all one would see.
Then did Moses the Law bring to Jews, but until the Law came
All man's sin was not charged; for man's sin did not yet have a name.

So from Genesis 12 to God's covenant with Abraham,
On to Isaac and Jacob and Joseph and Moses and then
On to Exodus thirty and four God gave Moses the Ten
Great Commandments. The Law was established and so was man's
sin.

Why did God put the Law in effect? It was added because
Of transgressions, until the seed came to whom the promise was
Duly made. In Galatians 3:19 to 24 we
Are told all are in need of a Saviour, whom Jesus Christ be.

Chapter 3 of Paul's letter to Romans, nineteen and beyond
To the twenty-eighth verse shows our needs were met. God did
respond.
We're made righteous by faith in Christ Jesus, without trying to
Fulfill all of the deeds of the law, which no man can thus do.

This book Romans reviews every aspect of what God has done
For His children. While we were yet sinners He gave us His son,
Who was crucified for our offenses and then raised again
For our justification. Belief in Him saves us from sin.

In Galatians 3 verse twenty-six and through to twenty-nine
Shows we all are included by faith in our Father's design.
So with Jesus, we're free from the law. He wants us to return
To God's mercy. Through Him we gain mercy that we did not earn.

37 *Foolish Galatians*

Please do *not* make the same mistake that the Galatians made. Paul
Called them "Foolish Galatians" for they had no concept at all
What it meant to be saved under Grace, for reverted they back
Under Law. They were cheating themselves. Understanding they
lacked.

In Galatians 3:1 to 3:14 Paul tried to explain
That the truth of the cross meant they're free. Did the Lord die in
vain?
They were blessed with the Spirit of God, as the promise was made
To their ancestor Abraham. His faith the foundation laid.

Paul does teach in Galatians 3:16, God's promise was to
Abraham and his "seed," not to "seeds." God meant Christ. He
would do
For us what the Law couldn't; give *LIFE*. We belong to Christ. We
Are thus heirs to the life that God promised. We're Abraham's seed.

So then is the Law bad? Is it sin? Romans 7 sheds light
On this matter. Verse five through verse eight explain we walk by
sight
When we're under the law, for it stirs up our passions and lusts
To want things that we shouldn't and we then ourselves cannot trust.

Let me give an example. If I told you not to look out
That far window, well until you looked, that's what you'd think about.

In Corinthians 15 and verse fifty-six we are told
That sin's strength is the law. The awareness of sin law does hold.

Chapter 7 of Romans, the end, Paul is frustrated. He
Feels he's trapped in the battle of flesh versus mind. But we see
Chapter 8 is the answer. The Spirit of God dwells in you,
So be mindful of Him. With His peace you'll be blessed through and
through.

A more excellent covenant gained we through Christ, as it states
In Paul's letter to Hebrews in verse six to twelve, chapter 8.
For the Lord put the law in our hearts, as it says in verse ten.
And verse twelve shows God's mercy. He will not remember our sin.

So then what does this mean for a Christian today? Well there are
Ways we put ourselves under the law without knowing how far
We have slipped. Through our personal guilt we condemn ourselves.
We
Also measure our efforts; not good enough. We are not free.

Is your emphasis on your performance? That's where you have failed
To be spiritually minded. It's not about you. You've derailed
His exceeding grace towards you. Your focus should be on the cross.
For it's all about Him and what He did. We gained from His loss.

So stop beating yourself up. In Romans 11 verse six
There's no question it's either by grace or by works; they don't mix.
We are joint heirs with Jesus, our Brother, and by His grace we
Are thus righteous through faith in His blood, and from works we
are free.

38 *Blessed vs Cursed*

There are very few Christians who truly know how to receive
All that's promised to them in the Bible. They try to achieve
Enough favor from God to be blessed, but results they don't get.
For we can't earn what's given; by faith we just need to accept.

Either that, or they just don't believe that they're righteous. For we
Are made righteous through Christ. It's a gift. We can't earn it. It's
free.
We are justified, "just as if" we never sinned. And unless
One's aware they're forgiven and righteous, they cannot be blessed.

In the seventeenth chapter, verse five to verse eight from the book
Jeremiah, we're given a vivid example. Let's look
At this bold explanation of how men should live. It contrasts
Both the man who is cursed to a man who is blessed to the last.

The man cursed in verse five, he's confounded by pride. In his own
Strength or effort he trusts; independent from God. He is shown
In verse six to be just like a shrub in the desert, for he
Is made blind by self-effort; when good comes he can't even see.

But verse seven shows blessed is the man who depends on the Lord.
He has good expectations, and good results are his reward.
He is blessed like a tree near the water. When heat or drought comes
He still prospers. He's thankful. He knows where his blessings are
from.

In verse ten is the proof, Psalm One Hundred and Three is not Old
Covenant; it's not Law. For this verse says that God does not hold
Sin against us. So Covenant truths from the New are contained
In this psalm. In verse three through verse five all our blessings are
named.

In Galatians 5:4 Paul does warn, don't go back under Law.
Once you're saved, trust in Jesus, not in your own efforts. Paul saw
Christians who were relying on works and self-effort to be
A success, and rejecting His grace. This will rob you. You're free.

In Galatians 3:10, once again is this curse mentioned. For
Then "As many" (it's your choice) as are under works, and ignore
The Lord's grace, they are cursed, by the Law (not by God). This
defends
Jeremiah and 17:5. Legalism condemns.

Verse eleven and twelve of Galatians 3 tell us the just
Live by faith, and that law is not faith. To be blessed then we must
Live by faith, that it might be by grace. Verse thirteen says that He,
By becoming a curse, from the curse of the law us redeemed.

Motivation's the difference. What causes one to do good deeds
Or good works? Well some do them because they are thankful you
see.
But if your motivation's to show others all that you do,
Or to earn God's acceptance, remember, it's not about you.

So much easier it would be just to lift hands to the Lord
And say, "Thank you for all of your blessings." We cannot afford

Not to recognize, He paid the price to redeem us. His grace
Is sufficient. Our future is bright and our past is erased.

You will lose at this life if you're focused on self. Only Him
Should your focus be on. If you focus on Jesus, you'll win.
Put your trust in the Lord and have faith in His promises, and
Your reward for your faith is the blessings of Old Abraham.

39 *Experience His Love*

In the Old Covenant, the Lord, He wrote the Law on two
Stone pieces. But in the New Covenant this would not do.
Inscribed He His law in our hearts. The old law cannot change
A person, but the new law can. Our minds get rearranged.

In Hebrews 8 verse ten to twelve, the Lord, He talks of the
New Covenant; "I'll put my laws into their mind," and He
Will be to us a God and we will be His people. We
Shall know Him and to our misconduct merciful He'll be.

Now notice in verse ten He says, "I'll put *my* laws into
Their mind." Not Moses' law. The law that He's referring to
Is not the Ten Commandments. So then what could these laws be?
The first is in John 13:34. It's love we see.

A new commandment gave He us. "Love one another." Yet
Not like we have loved in the past. Not carnal love. But let
Our love be *as* His love for us. In Romans chapter three
Verse twenty-seven, Jesus' other law is faith we see.

In Romans 3 verse 25 to 31 decrees
That man is justified by faith and not by works. So we
Conclude that faith in Jesus Christ is how we're justified,
Without obeying Ten Commandments; righteousness supplied.

Now laws are absolute. The law of electricity,
It works no matter what, in order, and consistently.
In feet per second squared we measure how fast gravity
Accelerates. It's constant for all masses, evenly.

You see, He's calling faith a law, and love a law. So we
Can know that these will work for us with regularity.
The trick is to receive His love and totally be free
Of works. Have faith in Jesus Christ. In His shed blood believe.

1 John 4:10, 11 and 19, "Herein is love;"
It's not that we loved God, but rather, first that He loved us,
And sent His Son as the Propitiation for our sins.
Redeemer, Arbitrator, Sacrifice; our souls He wins.

1 John 4:19 is the key. "We love him, (just) because
He first loved us." This Christian love's not "natural." It does
Not work unless one has an overwhelming and divine
Tuition, the "God loves me though I don't deserve it" kind.

Here is a famous verse, Ephesians 5 verse 25.
This verse, it gets taught wrong, for it says "Husbands, love your wives…"
Unless one first receives His love, they fail. It says to "do"
This thing; it's law. Now he must do it "for God told him to."

And also, First Corinthians 13, this chapter tells
Us all about what love should be and how it never fails.
Again this puts one under law. It can't be done unless
One first knows God loves them and with His love this person's blessed.

A spiritual principal is in Ephesians 3
And verse nineteen; "to *know* the love of Christ…that ye might be"
Filled with God's fullness. This word "know," it means "*experience*."
Perceive His love, the love *of* Christ. Observe it in this sense.

Experience His love. It is not human love. It does
Not look out for itself. It is not selfish; never was.
In Romans 13:10 it says that love the law fulfills.
Receive His love into your mind so you can do His will.

40 *The Mind of Christ*

Not one of us is privileged beyond our wildest dreams.
Success it does come easy to some people, so it seems.
But we don't know what they went through to get where they are
now.
The Holy Spirit wants to bless you if you will allow

Him and not quench Him. Train your mind to think on spiritual
things.
Your purpose is to gain the mind of Christ because He brings
You wisdom that's from God. Corinthians the First and two
Explains in detail what the mind of Christ can do for you.

Beloved know that neither eye nor ear has seen nor heard,
Nor entered in the heart of man the things that by God's word
Prepared He for all them that love Him. For He has revealed
Them to us by His Spirit. His own wisdom He does yield.

The worldly man does not receive the things the Spirit gives.
For they are foolishness to him; discerned by one who lives
For Jesus. As it says in First Corinthians and three,
The sixteenth verse, God's temple where His Spirit lives are we.

So what has God prepared for us? Each one of us must find
His will for us. It's personal. So learn to let your mind
Be guided by your Spirit, for God's Spirit lives in you.
So seek His will; discover what He has in store for you.

The key is in Corinthians the First and two, verse ten.
Revealed to us will be the wisdom of God's Spirit then.
So pray in your own personal prayer language, which you'll find
Allows you to know things beyond the limits of your mind.

So tap into the limitless supply of wisdom He
Will freely give to those who ask and seek. And what do we
Then have to lose, but time. Be patient. Wait upon the Lord.
The greatest wisdom that exists to us He will award.

41 *Tank Circuit*

So did you ever wonder how a radio picks up just one
Strong station at a time? Magnetic resonance is how it's done,
With a tank circuit. That's what's used to pick up just one frequency
While blocking all the others out. It's simple electricity.

The same it is when thinking of your soul, or mind, and how it's wired.
Is the tank circuit of your soul set to the frequency required
To thus receive the life of God and all His wisdom? It should pass
Right from your spirit to your mind without allowing static past.

The "static" is of course the stuff impeding your ability
To thus receive the life of God and all His wisdom that should be
Available to you because the Holy Spirit lives in you.
It's in your spirit that He lives. It's through your mind He talks to you.

Look at Ephesians 4 and verse eighteen where we are told why some
Are walking in the vanity of their own minds that's coming from
Their understanding being darkened. Alien are they to the
Life giving grace of God. Through ignorance they're blind and choose
to be.

So when you change your soul's tank circuit to be a good quality
Receiver, then as stated in Ephesians 4 verse twenty-three;
Your mind will be renewed. This war between your spirit and your soul
Is waging. Focus on the Lord and keep your mind in blessed control.

42 *Lukewarm*

'Tis better to be hot than cold, it's true.
To be on fire for God is good for you.
But even worse than cold is just lukewarm.
Unfortunately this is now the norm.

In Revelation 3 and verse fifteen
Through seventeen we learn what Jesus means
To be lukewarm. It's leaving Him on the
Outside, and living one's life separately.

Believing, but ignoring Him some go
About their business, rushing to and fro.
Such confidence they have in their own worth.
They have all that they need here on this earth.

Or so they think, but what about when they
Get caught up in life's snares. Well then they pray.
But that's ok. He's waiting patiently.
Just seek Him and He'll answer lovingly.

But knowest not that thou are wretched, poor,
And blind and naked. He waits at the door
And knocks. Verse twenty tells us if we hear
His voice and answer, then He will draw near.

All powerful, Almighty God is He.
And yet we all mean more to Him than we
Can even comprehend. If we could see
How much He loves us, then how blessed we'd be.

And so without Him, we are lost as sheep
Without a Shepherd. By ourselves we'll reap
Life's hardships. So 'tis better to be hot
Than cold, or worse, lukewarm. Ignore Him not.

43 *The Mother of Jesus*

"…Blessed art thou among women," is what Mary heard
In Luke 1:28 from the angel of God who gave word
To this faithful young virgin. The following verses record
How her favor with God made her mother of Jesus, our Lord.

Such great things she was told about Jesus. Did she understand
What was meant when informed "of His kingdom there shall be no end?"
When the babe in Elisabeth's womb leaped for joy at her hail,
Mary knew that she carried the Saviour of all Israel.

In Luke 2 verses twenty-two through thirty-eight there were two
Elder servants of God; Simeon and then Anna who knew
That this babe who was brought to the temple indeed was the One;
The Lord's Christ God had sent to the world. His life had just begun.

This was not the first, nor the last time Mary marveled at those
Things that others had said about Jesus her son. But suppose
That as days and years slowly crept by, to forget one would start.
She was raising the Christ; and these things she did keep in her heart.

One can only imagine that Jesus was the sweetest child
One could ever endeavor to raise. Was He gentle and mild?
After giving His parents a scare at age 12 in Luke 2,
He thereafter remained subject unto them throughout His youth.

The first miracle Jesus performed was at the beckoning
Of His mother who urged Him in John 2 verse 3 this wedding
Was in danger of losing its blessing; no wine was at hand.
For she knew He could fix it. The servants obeyed His command.

In the end she could not comprehend why her son had to die.
Nothing that she could do. He died willingly for all mankind.
Oh the anguish of watching Him suffering there on the cross.
She would later rejoice. Life and peace gained the world from her loss.

Thus the prophecy Mary did speak of herself has come true.
That from henceforth all people would recognize her blessings due,
As she said in Luke 1:48. And to all who believe
In Lord Jesus, such wonderful blessings we all do receive.

44 *The Virgin Birth*

The miracle of Jesus' birth is not the day that He was born,
Which most of us, as Christians, celebrate each year on Christmas
morn.
The Bible shows us three events that prove December 25th
Is when the Virgin Mary did conceive the Lord; God's perfect gift.

The first is John the Baptist. Six months older than the Lord was he.
In Luke and chapter one it tells the story of how blessed he'd be.
His father, Zacharias was a temple priest. An angel came
To tell him he would have a son of greatness; John would be his
name.

John's father did complete his course; Abia on June 19th, then
The next day was the Sabbath. After that he traveled home again.
So on about June 24th Elisabeth his wife became
Then pregnant with their son, just as the angel Gabriel did claim.

In Luke verse twenty-six we see that when Elisabeth was in
The sixth month of her pregnancy, then Gabriel did move again.
It now was Mary's turn. He told her that the Holy Ghost would come
To make her pregnant with Lord Jesus. He would be God's only Son.

The shepherds, they were in the fields when angels from above
proclaimed
The birth of Jesus Christ the Lord. Luke 2, ten to fourteen is famed.

And to this day, the shepherds with their flocks are never out at the
Year's end. Too cold it is. October is the latest out they'll be.

September 29th for Jesus' birth is a much truer date.
In John 1:14 it does say, "The word (that's Jesus, He) was made
(Of) flesh, and dwelt among us." Tabernacled is the word for "dwelt."
The Feast of Tabernacles is the time of Jesus' birth, it's felt.

Born in a manger was the Lord, for no room at an inn was there.
This "Tabernacle" feast required that all male Jews did come to where
The feast was taking place; Jerusalem. And Bethlehem was near.
And also, Romans, during such a feast would schedule tax time here.

So what we celebrate, the miracle of Jesus' birth, it is
In fact the miracle of His "conception." So just think of this
Date that we glorify the Lord, December 25th, as the
Most perfect date that we could honor God's gift of Eternity.

45 *Greater than John*

John the Baptist was greater than all other men in the Old
Testament. In Luke 1, sixty-six to verse eighty we're told
Of his stature and influence. He would make ready the way
For the Lord. His whole life he did spend to prepare for that day.

Now in Matthew 11:11 'twas Jesus who said
John was greater than all born of women. But notice instead
Of his greatness persisting today, anyone who has been
Thus born into the kingdom of heaven is greater than him.

Even he who is "least" in the kingdom of heaven has more
Than John ever did have in that day. And here's why, to be sure.
Once the Lord gave His life and ascended to heaven, all who
Thus believe in Him gain in their spirits the Holy Ghost too.

For the Kingdom of Heaven on earth is us Christians. We are
The vast body of Christ. We have God in our spirits. By far
We have quite the advantage. As Paul says, Christ lives in us. We
Have more than the Old Testament saints, to the millionth degree.

But what made John so great? He did not cast out devils, nor was
He thus used by God to heal the sick. Well suppose that because
He abstained from most, if not all pleasures, this made him grow
strong.
And the Holy Ghost, He was "upon" him for all his life long.

To ignore your own body, it makes you much stronger you see.
John the Baptist spent years with the Lord in the wilderness. He
Did live simply, on honey and locusts. He fasted and prayed.
And he read, for he quoted Isaiah. Devout were his days.

In Luke 1 verse sixteen and verse seventeen Gabriel told
Zacharias, John's father, that John would be guilelessly bold
Like Elijah. He'd turn hearts of fathers to children and he
Would make ready a people prepared for the Lord, he decreed.

In Isaiah and 40 shows John was the voice who was sent;
Who did cry in the wilderness, watch for the Lord and repent.
John did not strive to be better than the Lord. He knew his worth.
The baptism of Jesus Christ was his great purpose on earth.

You should never degrade your position in Christ. Just receive
Revelation that all things are possible when you believe.
In Ephesians and 1 we're informed we are all greatly blessed;
Highly favored, forgiven and loved. We are His righteousness.

46 *Heaven and Earth*

"Heaven," by Randy Alcorn, the source for this poem,
is the most accurate book in existence describing Heaven,
based firmly on scripture. Dr. Alcorn's Eternal
Perspective Ministries website is www.epm.org.

As believers, we're told in Colossians 3:2 not to set
Our affections on things on the earth, but above. We're to get
Rid of worldly desires, for we now are in Christ, and thus we
Are His heirs in this life, and in Heaven His bride we will be.

Now have you ever wondered what life here on earth would have
been
Like if Adam and Eve had not fallen and there was no sin?
Well the scriptures do indicate that God's original plan
For His children to live on this earth will be realized again.

This will happen when Jesus returns, and the New Earth ensues;
All the good and the beauty of old earth, but better, renewed.
There will be no more death or despair, nor the evils of sin.
Man will be resurrected to reign on this earth once again.

Now the devil, he wants you to think that your heavenly home
Is a place of sheer boredom, and as a ghost floating you'll roam.
But this couldn't be further from truth. There is both time and space
In the Heaven that's Present. Though not the New Earth, it's a place.

In the meanwhile, you will have a body, and you will be you.
You'll be recognized by all your loved ones, and you'll know them too.
All your memories and all the good things you did will persist.
But the fears and the doubts and the anguish no longer exist.

In Isaiah the sixtieth chapter the prophet explains
A great scene of a glorified city built on the remains
Of old earth. He describes this vast city on New Earth as the
Lord's New Heaven, where there will be eternal excellency.

Revelation's last chapters both also describe this same sight.
It is named New Jerusalem, and down from heaven it lights
On New Earth. Here our God will dwell with all His people, and they
Will enjoy no more sorrow or pain, which has all passed away.

All God's creatures, the animals, they'll be redeemed and alive.
As it says in Isaiah the sixty-fifth, verse twenty-five,
They will not harm each other; on earth's vegetation they'll graze.
They will frolic and play and delight us in all of their ways.

And in our resurrected new bodies, we'll play with them too.
We'll be healthy and strong and have stamina for all we do.
Will we sleep? I don't know. But the Book says that there will be
feasts.
Not to mention our wedding to Jesus; now there we'll surfeit.

I suppose there will be no more gluttony, oh but how we
Love to eat. And can you just imagine how "heavenly" the
Food in Heaven will taste? We'll indulge all we want and not gain
Any weight. We will not eat to live, but the pleasure remains.

Now in heaven we will not be married. Collectively we
Will all be Jesus' bride, but that doesn't mean we will not be
With the ones that we loved here on earth. Even Adam's wife Eve
God had made so he'd be not alone. Social creatures are we.

For a marriage on earth to be happy, successful and blessed,
Both its partners draw near to the Lord, and the closer they get
To the Lord then the closer they'll get to each other. So this
Institution on earth does prepare us for heavenly bliss.

Is there anyone famous in Heaven who you'd like to see?
Like someone from the Bible who first hand knows its history.
Though the One who engages us most; Who we'll most want to
spend
Our time with is the Master Himself. He'll be our closest Friend.

On New Earth we'll be busy, with work and with learning and more.
The whole earth, and the vast universe will be ours to explore.
There's no end to adventures we'll have, and we'll have endless time
To enjoy our new life on New Earth. Heaven will be sublime.

So the Jews who believed the Messiah would come to restore
All their people as well as Jerusalem, which they adored,
Could have never expected God's plan of redemption to be
One encompassing ALL of creation for eternity.

We are made in God's image, but finite, and physical too.
And the God-Man, our groom has a body, the same as we do.
So to quote Randy Alcorn's great book of our future, "We're made
For a person, King Jesus; and also for Heaven, the place."

47 *Self-Centered*

We are taught all our lives to be focused on "Me."
Go to school. Get good grades. Be the best you can be.
Strive for wealth. Treat yourself. To your own self be true.
Look your best and be proud. Make the world notice you.

So the two or three hours of most weeks that we spend
In our church does not compensate for this "Me" trend.
And the pastor is faced with the difficult chore
Of diverting our focus to things that mean more.

But what happens to people when they only think
About their own desires for success? Well they sink
In their failure to reach their own personal best.
If you focus on self you will end up depressed.

For this self-love is empty, and time will erase
Your achievements and goals. They will pale in the face
Of your age and your losses. But His love you see
Can fill in all the holes, and fulfilled you will be.

This does not mean that you should avoid any fame
Or success the Lord blesses you with. But His name
Put ye first. Give Him thanks for His goodness to you.
When we give God the glory, success will ring true.

So when raising your kids, teach them how to depend
On their Lord. More important is this than the trend
Of the worldly achievements we push on our youth.
To be joyful in life we must all seek God's truth.

48 *Christ Centered*

When you are focused on the Lord, in "perfect peace" your mind
Will rest.
Isaiah 26 verse three confirms this truth. His very best
Is yours, so just accept His blessings. But for some it's not so plain.
They feel they need to earn His gift, and for their efforts nothing gain.

Corinthians the Second, chapter three and verse eighteen defines
What happens when His glory you behold; He then does change your
mind
Into His very image. It's as if you're looking in a mirror,
And staring back at you is Him; His peace, His love, His lack of fear.

This means that you'll be humble, but you won't a doormat be. And
you
Will become bold, but you won't feel superior. You'll just want to
Impart to others what you've learned with confidence. You'll have
no shame
When sharing His "good news" with others; how you're blessed, in
Jesus' name.

Corinthians the Second, chapter ten verse three through five does
make
It clear that you are in a war that's spiritual. Make no mistake;
The battle's in your mind. You fight with weapons that aren't natural,
But mighty through your God to pull down strongholds that would
make you fall.

Verse five explains that you must bring your thoughts into captivity,

Through Christ. You need His help, although the battle's yours. So you can see

That casting out imaginations and the high things that impede

Your peace from God is vital to your mental health. He's all you need.

Philippians 4:8 will tell you whatsoever things are true,

And honest, just and pure and lovely, praiseworthy, and things that do

Have virtue, are of good report; these are the things on which you should

Be thinking. If your thoughts do not match these things then they are no good.

Get rid of them! Just cast them out. The "high things" that must leave your mind

Are selfishness and unforgiveness; hateful thoughts, they'll rob you blind.

And also fears and doubts and information that's not true will make

Your mind a mess. Protect your mind. Your happiness is what's at stake.

In Romans chapter seven, verse eighteen to twenty-five is where

Paul tells us when his focus is on Christ, he is without a care.

But when his focus is on "I" and "me," as you will see all through

These verses, then his mind's at odds against his flesh. The war ensues.

And then in Romans 8 verse one, Paul has a revelation of

The Lord and what it means for Christ to be in him; His peace and love

Are in Paul's mind. There is no condemnation now, and for all time
For Paul, or anyone who recognizes Christ is in their mind.

No condemnation "now" means from the moment that we sin we are
Forgiven. Romans 8 verse thirty-five through thirty-nine by far
Do show us how much we are loved; and nothing shall thus separate
Us from the love of God through Jesus Christ our Lord. On us He
waits.

Ephesians 1 verse three through seven tell us we're already blessed.
All spiritual blessings do belong to us, so we can rest
In knowing that we are accepted; highly favored by His grace.
You didn't earn it. Just receive it. His pure love for you embrace.

Whose job is it to keep your mind on Christ? It's yours, so learn to let
Your mind be guided by your spirit, where He lives. Then you will get
A revelation of His presence in your mind, and you'll be free
From ugly thoughts that subjugate your mind, and you'll have perfect
peace.

49 *Where is Your Focus?*

We all face circumstances that are for the most part way beyond
Our own control. Important is the way we cope. One can respond
With worry or with negativity and claim an outcome bad.
It doesn't have to be like that. To prophecy defeat is sad.

Where is your focus? Where's your faith? When you're confronted
with distress,
Is God your source? He should be. He knows every detail of your
mess.
Let's follow the example of the Lord Himself. The battle He
Did face, it was the Battle of the Ages. Surely you'll agree.

Now men who go to war, though they don't know the outcome, they
have hope
That they will make it. And this gives them courage. But the Lord a
rope
He had around His neck. He knew exactly what hell He would face.
He knew His purpose on this earth was death, to save the human
race.

And not just any death. A brutal death. One most could not explain,
Or even comprehend. He as our Substitute endured much pain
Excruciating; not just stripes upon His back or being nailed.
The worst were sins and sicknesses His flesh upon that cross assailed.

Before He took on flesh, He was "The Word." So Jesus knew about
Isaiah 53; He authored it. He also had no doubt
That He'd experience what David wrote in both Psalm 22
And 69; His prayers while on the cross and in the garden too.

Right after the Last Supper, Matthew 26 verse thirty-one,
The Lord told His disciples they'd abandon Him 'til all was done,
Just as was prophesied in Zechariah 13:7. At
The Garden of Gethsemane He prayed while His disciples sat.

His closest three disciples He took with Him; Peter, James and John.
He told them how His heart was heavy; asked them to stand watch
beyond.
In Matthew 26 verse thirty-nine He begged His Father, "...let
This cup pass from me..." for His thinking was not clear, nor
strengthened yet.

He knew this was the only way. Remember, Jesus, He was just
A man, a human, flesh and bone, in all points tempted just like us.
He needed strength and courage yet to face this trial. Verse forty-two
Says when He prayed again He was accepting of what He must do.

A third time He did pray, and gained the fortitude to do what He
Knew would redeem us all; the Father's will. Now for eternity
We have the same advantage Jesus had. He made us good enough
To boldly come unto the throne of God for help when times are tough.

50 *The Name of Jesus*

There's a colon misplaced that's in Mark 16 verse seventeen.
The original Greek did not have all these marks that are seen.
Punctuation was added in later to clarify text.
Here is why this said colon should be to the right, three words next.

This verse says in King James, "And these signs (they) shall follow (all) them
That believe; in my name shall they…" do all the things the Lord came
For to show us. In Matthew's last chapter, in the eighteenth verse
Says "…All power is given to (Jesus) in heaven and earth."

And that power He gives to us all. The authority He
Has to make devils leave human bodies, and more, so do we.
For it says in 1 John chapter 4:17, "…as He is,
So are we in this world," all because our Lord Jesus, He lives.

He needs us, in our physical bodies performing His will
Here on earth, for He now is a Spirit, no longer fulfills
He the requisite. We are His body, the church. He's the head.
When a devil looks into your eyes, they do see God instead.

But believing in Him, by itself does not give us His grit.
We must be baptized into His might by the Holy Spirit.
No one who just believes in the Lord has the power to lay
Both their hands on the sick for to have them recover this way.

The beginning of this dispensation which we are now in
Was in Acts chapter two, after Pentecost. Peter therein
Did give boldly a speech that explained these new tongues they all had.
Then more people were saved and got the Holy Ghost and were glad.

And all through this book Acts, when a person got saved and believed
In Lord Jesus, the very next thing that they did was receive
The baptism of the Holy Ghost. This is how it was done.
But in two thousand years, look how far from this habit we've come.

This book Acts, it was never "completed," we may in truth say.
For this book of the Bible is still being "written" today.
We are still all the "church" of the Lord, and we still have the same
Command from our Lord Jesus to "go" and perform in His name.

The first verse that was mentioned that's in Mark 16, it should say,
"And these signs (they) shall follow (all) them who believe in my
name;..."
It's His name that gives us the authority to go and do
Whatsoever the Spirit, whose might we now have, asks us to.

51 *Unbroken Fellowship*

A most confusing passage in the Bible is 1 John 1:9.
It leads one to believe confessing sins is needed all the time.
But what we must consider is the audience John wrote this to.
It's written to agnostics who do not believe that God is true.

But just two passages away; 1 John 1:7 it decrees
That if we walk in Jesus' light as He is in the light, then we
Have fellowship with one another, and the blood of Jesus Christ,
God's Son, it cleanses us entirely from sin. It does suffice.

Thus walking in His light is just believing Jesus is the Son
Of God who took on flesh and died, and rose again; the only One
Who qualified to be our Substitute for sin. He paid our debt.
And knowing that we're loved by our Creator's the best feeling yet.

In this verse, "cleanse" is in the present tense. It is continual.
We're washed in an unending downpour of Christ's blood which makes us all
His righteousness. And so our fellowship with Him we cannot lose.
Unbroken fellowship with God for life is ours once Him we choose.

52 *It All Makes Sense*

It all makes perfect sense when we consider just how similar
Historically the strongest two religions of the world they are.
Two different paths they took, and yet they have the same beginnings.
They
Both honor God of Abraham, and He's their One True God today.

The Muslims call Him "Allah." "Father God" in Heaven Christians
call
Him. The Koran does speak of Jesus, and its' passages recall
Validity of both the Torah and the Gospel. It reveals
Mohammad said himself to trust the Bible's truth, so he appealed.

The Bible, it was "penned" by over forty men from every walk
Of life, and covered fifteen hundred years, and yet no doubt it talks
Of one main Character, Messiah Jesus, and consistently
It holds the theme of God's plan of redemption for eternity.

In contrast, the Koran it was compiled from what was thought to be
The revelations of Mohammad found on scraps years after he
Expired. Mohammad walked the earth from five hundred and seventy
A.D. He unified Arabia under one polity.

Islam, it goes one step beyond the Jews who don't believe in the
Messiah, Jesus. The Koran does indicate that Jesus, He's
The "Word" of God, and testifies of miracles that He performed.
And yet it does deny that He's the Son of God; it misinforms.

A Muslim who is raised a Muslim has no choice. They must "believe"
The Laws of the Koran and all its precepts, or the penalty
Is death. It teaches all are slaves to Allah, and it does condone
The killing of all unbelievers; tolerates none but their own.

Sharia Law, the law that Muslims follow, it is not contained
In the Koran, but in the Hadith, written by the Muslims famed
For being scholars. This is their interpretation of what they
Supposed Mohammad wished for all his followers until this day.

If one does read in the Old Testament the Books of Moses, they
Will see that God's Laws first imposed on Jews were strict, and they
did pay
A penalty of death quite often for their sins. How can one not
Thus see that this is where Sharia Law, both fierce and swift, was got.

In Deuteronomy and 21, eighteen to twenty-one
It shows what would have happened in the Law unto a wayward son.
And such a son does Jesus thus describe in Luke 15, but He
Does give a different outcome of the prodigal son's fate, we see.

For in the Law, this son described in verse eleven to nineteen
Would have been stoned to death. His bad behavior, it would have
been seen
As unforgivable. And yet the father in this story, he
Did have compassion on his son, rejoicing his return with glee.

So in this story of a loving father, Jesus shows us how
Our Father, God in Heaven, loves us more than our brains will allow
Us all to comprehend. For Jesus, up until He died was in
A pre-cross world, and yet His parables they told of post-cross sin.

For Jesus knew His purpose. He knew Father God would nail the Law
Unto His cross with Him, and Grace would then replace it. Jesus saw
The world as it would be, and so His stories did reflect His grace.
A post-cross man was Jesus in a pre-cross world that He did face.

So understand, this picture Jesus gives of Father God is one
Of Love. While we were all yet sinners, God He gave His only Son
To die for us. Messiah's death upon the cross redeemed us to
Our Father God in Heaven, for our debt is paid. We've been made new.

So we can see that Satan, the deceiver, he did pretty well
Convincing men to follow this false prophet, leading men to hell.
In less than just two centuries the devil did corrupt a vast
Amount of people on the earth. He will not give up 'til the last.

But Father God, He knows our hearts. Salvation is a matter He
Does leave up to each person, and no one can force their own beliefs
On others. That's the devil's way. But God loves us so much that He
Gives us the choice to love Him back. We must choose individually.

53 *Jesus in the Koran*

In the holy Koran there are six thousand, six hundred sixty-six
words.

And believe it or not, it does talk about Jesus, yet nothing was heard
Until recently how it proclaims His importance. So let me relate
The bold story of Mario Joseph, whose life was so twisted by fate.

His dear mother was sick when she carried him. She was advised to
abort
Him. But she would not hear of it. She prayed to Allah and asked
him, in short,
For the life of her child. In return she would "give" him to Allah, so
he
Was raised Muslim in India and he became an Imam finally.

And while preaching to Muslims, someone in the crowd asked him
who is this man
They call Jesus? So looking for answers he read the entire Koran.
The Koran mentions Jesus in twenty-five places, but only four times
Does it mention Mohammad. Confused he was by this surprise he
did find.

Then ten points he discovered about Jesus Christ in the holy Koran.
There are three names for Jesus it gives; "Word of God" was the first
that he ran
Into. Also it calls Jesus "Spirit of God." "Jesus Christ" is the last.
Many wonderful things it does say about Him and His life in the past.

Jesus spoke as a baby, and also He made a live bird out of clay.
This excited young Mario. Jesus breathed life and the bird flew away.
Jesus also cured blindness and healed leprosy, and from death He
raised men.
And He did go to Heaven; He is still alive, and He will come again.

He was still not convinced that this Jesus was more than a prophet,
although
When compared to Mohammad, He's greater indeed. The Koran told
him so.
For the prophet Mohammad did none of these things and had none
of these names.
Plus he died, he's still dead, and he's not coming back, as the story
remains.

Then he asked his one teacher, "How did God create the vast
universe?" And
His instructor's reply was that God spoke it into existence, again,
"Through the Word." So the critical question for Mario now was, the
"word,"
Did this mean the "Creator?" Or rather "Creation," which would be
absurd.

If he answered "Creator," then this meant that Jesus, who the Koran
names
As the "word" is thus God, and all Muslims must then become
Christians. The game
Is then over. "Creation," how can it create? So he stubbornly said
That the word is thus "neither," refusing to answer this question
instead.

Well the teacher was angry and made him depart. So he put his Koran

To his chest and he prayed asking Allah to show him what should he do then.

When he opened the book he saw verse ninety-four chapter ten which did say,

If there be any doubts, then the Bible is clear. (Jesus Christ is the way.)

He decided to study the Bible, and went to a Catholic retreat.

He was pleased that the Bible was similar to the Koran. They did meet.

In particular John's first few verses confirmed Jesus Christ is the word.

But what touched him was John and verse twelve. Truly this he had not before heard.

For it says in this verse that all those who receive Jesus Christ have the power

To become sons of God. This he could not ignore. He became in this hour

A true Christian. To call God his "daddy," this gave him unspeakable joy.

So began his devotion to Jesus. A fellowship none could destroy.

For in contrast, a Muslim is slave to their Allah, and master is he.

And a slave, he does not love his master, nor master his slave. So you see

That a man-made religion can never compare to the power of God's love.

He gives life and His peace. So accept this true love from your Father above.

54 *Fading Flower*

Our nation is a fading flower, like the Israel of old;
Once boundless, now declining towards a state of ruin, truth be told.
How can this be? For "We the People" founded this great nation on
Our trust in God, and He has blessed it powerfully since its dawn.

The only other nation that was founded on belief in One
True God, the God of Abraham is Israel. But God's own Son,
Named Jesus Christ they do not honor. That is where we differ. The
United States, its constitution's based on Christianity.

Our Founding Fathers knew that men in roles of leadership can be
Thus influenced by evil, so they prayed before completing the
Bold Constitution, giving it a balance of three powers. They
Used the example of the Father, Son and Holy Ghost we'd say.

So where did we go wrong? Well time it took for Satan's influence
To root and grow. He only needed to corrupt our innocence.
He started with the family. No longer stable is this part
Of life in wonderful America. He choked us at the heart.

Prosperity is also a strong factor. No one has the time
To spend with God, if they were even taught to seek His will. The
crime
Of making all else in one's life of more importance than the Lord,
Like education, work and recreation, we cannot afford.

Let's look at the example in the Bible of the other folks
Whose nation honored God. In several chapters of Isaiah spoke
The prophet of God's judgment on Jerusalem. In 28
Verse one God warns of pride. A fading flower those who once were
great.

Isaiah 30 warns that they did not take counsel of the Lord.
Instead they did rebel and put their trust in strength of man. Toward
The shadow, Egypt, they did look with confidence; to this their
shame.
When "government" becomes one's source then trouble's only theirs
to blame.

And so we too have walked away from our first love. We put our
trust
In man and government, and not in God, and even tried to thrust
Him out. And what a mess we have. Too many hands do stir the pot.
The right does not know what the left is doing. God knows, but He's
not

Respected, sought or counseled. Second Timothy and chapter three,
Verse one through five is coming true today. And know this
prophecy
Will thus continue. There is nothing we can do to stop it. So
What can we do? Let's put our trust in God and help His kingdom
grow.

God's answer is in Titus 2:11 and verse 12. His grace,
Does teach us to deny ungodliness and worldly lusts. His face
We seek, for through his grace we'll shine with righteousness, and
soberly
We'll live as Godly children in this present world, for all to see.

55 *One Nation Under God*

One may think 9/11 was God's judgment on us, but no.
It was not. Revelation's when God will judge all the earth so,
So severely. The "absence" of God is what hurt us that day.
For our hedge of protection from God's slowly going away.

Well, what did we expect? As a nation we no longer seek
God's protection or strength. We are prideful and no longer meek.
In fact, we kicked Him out of our government; out of our schools.
God will not be where He is not wanted. One could call us "fools."

God's not judging America. He blessed this nation because
We once honored Him. Many still do, although fewer, but does
Our voice count? Well of course it does. He loves us. But we must
pray.
Let us pray for God's blessings restored on this nation today.

56 *Serve Your Employer*

Being blessed at your job's not as hard as you guess.
There is one foolproof way that won't cause you distress.
All you do is adhere to the Bible's advice.
In Ephesians 6:5 it is all summed up nice.

Now you'll notice this verse says for servants to be
As obedient to their own masters as we
Are to Christ. So how does this apply to today?
Well employees should serve their employers this way.

It matters not if one's employer's a schmuck.
There will always be those no one wants to get stuck
Working for. But remember it's Christ who you serve,
So let's give Him our best which is what He deserves.

When you learn to adopt such a good attitude
You'll be pleasantly free and in such a great mood
At your workplace, and don't be surprised when you're blessed
With rewards. That's what happens when we give our best.

57 *Wisdom's Warnings*

The first eleven chapters that wise Solomon composed
In Proverbs are about God's wisdom. Everyone should know
That wisdom is more valuable than gold and silver. We
Can learn so much from Wisdom. She's a Personality.

In Proverbs chapter eight is wisdom called a "she." She warns
Us all to choose the path that's right. All evil ways she scorns.
In verses twenty-two through thirty-one it does appear
That Wisdom and the Lord are One; profound's this proverb here.

In Proverbs 5, verse seven to thirteen does Wisdom warn
At off-ramps on your path. She warns, "Do not get off." Forlorn
You'll be. Verse twelve shows pride will trip you up, if you do hate
To be instructed or reproved. Wake up. Don't be irate.

In Proverbs 8 again, verse twenty, Wisdom leads the way
In righteousness. Verse twenty-one, to love her it does say,
Will bring one blessings. Proverbs 10 verse twelve ensures that love
Does cover up all sins. Seek first life's treasures from above.

58 How to Choose

In Romans 12, verse one and two it tells us how to live
Like we have been made new. Verse one informs us we should give
Our bodies as a holy, living sacrifice to Him.
In other words, don't let your flesh live out it's selfish whims.

Control your flesh. Whatever you do with your body, He
Does with you. He lives in you. Drinking, drugs and all He sees.
Immediately He forgives you, but can you forgive
Yourself? You have defiled His home. Don't trash the place He lives.

Verse two says do not be conformed to worldly ways, but be
Transformed by the renewing of your mind. Not you, but He
Renews your mind when you spend time with Him, in prayer or
thought.
This practice of His presence lets Him know His will you've sought.

Then you'll have no desire to get caught up in any mess
That those who seek the world are in, and with His peace He'll bless
Your mind. Colossians 1 verse 12 Paul thanks our Father who
Has made us qualified to be partakers of this new

Life whereby we can know that we are righteous, just because
Of His son Jesus' death upon the cross for us. It does
Help also when we know that Wisdom cries to us. Verse four
Of Proverbs 8 does tell us Wisdom calls to us. Be sure

And understand that Wisdom's always speaking to you. When
You take an unwise detour from your chosen path, well then
You'll hear from Wisdom. Seek her, for verse seventeen does say
That She loves those who love her back. She'll guide you on your way.

In Proverbs 15:2 we see that knowledge does depend
On Wisdom to be used correctly. Wisdom is your friend.
Increase your knowledge, giving Wisdom opportunity
To guide your mind. She'll keep you on the lighted path. You'll see.

In Proverbs 4, verse twenty-three through twenty-six we're told
To keep our hearts with diligence. This means do not behold
Just anything. Protect your mind. Be choosy what you see
And hear. Yes "ponder," think about the person you will be.

Don't be impulsive. Think about the path your feet will take.
For happy is the man, or woman, who finds Wisdom. Make
Sure that you understand that wisdom's "hearing" from the Lord;
And honor, wealth and length of days from Him is your reward.

If you need proof of this, it says it right in Proverbs 3,
Verse thirteen through to eighteen, which says Wisdom is a tree
Of life to those that seek her. She's your source. Verse nineteen states
The Lord used Wisdom to create the earth and heavens great.

There is one "catch" to Wisdom speaking to you. You must "hear"
What Wisdom says. To gain her is to have a "hearing ear."
You cannot hear her when you fill your mind with other stuff,
Like TV, radio or noise. There is not room enough.

So meditate, yes "meditate." This means to mutter to
Yourself while thinking. Read the Bible. Put yourself into
The story, like the woman who was healed in Matthew 9.
For she believed if she touched Jesus' garment she'd be fine.

A powerful and mighty verse is Joshua 1:8.
The Lord told Joshua, both day and night to meditate.
Let not His word depart from him. The Law to him's the same
As Jesus' word to us. We have success, in Jesus' name.

The promises to us, the church of Jesus Christ, are great.
They're better than the Covenant in Joshua 1:8.
The Bible will empower you to be a doer of
His word. He'll put His laws into your heart; His faith and love.

So choose to listen to the Holy Spirit, and allow
His word to change you. Meditating on His word is how
We can be changed by Him. Your time; that's all He needs from you.
Devote your time to Him and He will bless you through and through.

59 *King Asa*

Let us look at the life of King Asa, who started out on
The right path. Second Chronicles chapter fourteen and verse one
Through verse five show for ten years he did what was good in the
eyes
Of the Lord. And God blessed him with peace in the land. Recognize

How he dealt with disaster. Verse nine shows an armament came
To attack him. A million-man army they faced, but God's name
He did call upon in verse eleven. He knew that for Him
This was nothing. He knew if they'd trust in God's help they would
win.

Now remember, this story's Old Testament. Jesus had not
Died yet for us. In chapter fifteen and verse two, if they sought
The Lord then He'd be with them, "but if ye forsake him" He would
Forsake them. In verse eight, Asa heeded these words and felt good.

He took courage in knowing that God was thus with him. It does
Take much courage to be a committed strong Christian because
One must exercise faith and not walk by one's sight. Faith is rest.
Trust in God is to rest in His might; not to worry or fret.

Chapter sixteen begins Asa's downfall. Verse one to verse three
Shows how Asa did pay for a victory. He did not "need"
Help from God. One can see that his judgment was clouded by pride.
He no longer depended on God. He just put Him aside.

In verse seven to ten a new seer informed Asa that
He'd have wars from then on for this foolish mistake. And then at
The last years of his reign, when his feet were diseased, once again
He did not seek the Lord, but physicians, and thus met his end.

Now this story of Asa the king can be useful to we
Who are governed by Grace. In the New Covenant we are free.
God will not make us pay when we don't honor Him and first seek
His will for us. But stories like these show us where we are weak.

For to honor the Lord and to trust Him is priceless, and we
Cannot find any better prescription or habit to be
A success in this life. Seek Him first and all else will thus fall
Into place. It takes courage; have faith in Him. Answer your call.

60 *We "Agnostics"*

In the wonderful book, "Alcoholics Anonymous" there's
Chapter four, a most eloquent, logical memoir which dares
To thus challenge agnostics who suffer from this grave disease
To consider a broader opinion; to change their beliefs.

For this alcoholism is the most destructive of ills.
And its victims are prey to depression and misery. Still
They've a chance if they're honest, admitting that they cannot beat
This alone. This is their only hope this disease to defeat.

So encouraged are they to accept an alternative to
Being doomed to a certain cruel death. They need only pursue
Something greater than their own resources which utterly failed.
If they'd trust in a Power that's greater than them, they'd prevail.

For as soon as they laid aside prejudice; opened their minds
To the possible truth of this Power that's greater in kind
Than themselves, then they did get results, even though they did not
Comprehend fully yet that this force was the Spirit of God.

Much to their own relief they did not need adopt others' views
About God. Just a simple approach to make contact would do.
For the Realm of the Spirit is never exclusive. He gives
All who seek Him a welcoming chance to accept Him and live.

This beginning of spiritual growth was the start of a new
Way of living and thinking. The question of faith brought them to
"God-sufficiency." It really works. All the answers can't be
Found in reason or logical things. Faith is what makes one free.

61 *Hearing From God*

If you're spiritually minded, then you're open to
Thoughts from God. He will guide you in all that you do.
Now you probably will not hear God audibly.
You'll get promptings, or "nudges" from Him frequently.

You will sense that these nudges are good. They're the right
Thing to do, or to not. Avoid walking by sight.
And these "red lights" or "green lights" you get, they can be
Vital. He cares about you; your every need.

In the Book of Acts, Jesus' Apostles, they learned
To take heed of these promptings their spirits discerned.
Paul in Acts 27:10 said "...I perceive
That this voyage will be" with much hurt, he believed.

He was right. He perceived in his spirit that they
Would have trouble. They did. And so this is the way
That God "talks" to us, mostly. A vision sometimes
One will have, just like Paul in Acts 16 verse nine.

This book Acts, it describes the first "church" of Christ. The
Holy Ghost, He lives in us and guides us if we
Learn to "listen." These were the first Christians to do
What the Holy Ghost prompted. They knew they were "new."

Even Jesus, He had a flesh body; a Man.
The first Man to have God in His spirit. So then
He perceived just like us, in His spirit. Said He
In Luke 8:48, "virtue's gone out of me."

John 16's where the Lord told us why He must die.
He redeemed us to God and He did not deny
Us the chance for our spirits to quicken with the
Holy Ghost. Now we too have God in us, like He.

In verse seven He said, "If I go not away"
Then the Comforter would not be with us to stay.
Verse thirteen says, "…He will shew you things (yet) to come."
Now we know what He meant; Who these nudges are from.

Read the rest of the Acts. More examples you'll see
Of how God talks to us supernaturally.
Seek ye Him and be spiritually minded, and you
Will perceive then His guidance. He'll broaden your view.

62 *Believe*

For those who know that Jesus is the Son
Of God through whom our righteousness is won,
Who walk in expectation of the best;
They understand it's God who gives them rest.

The trick you see is that their minds were changed.
Priorities of theirs were rearranged.
And when no longer former lusts remain,
They realize to lose the world is gain.

For in God's word their minds choose to believe.
And thus the promises of God receive.
In Thessalonians the first and two
Thirteen, tells how your mind can be changed too.

Effective is the word of God when you
Believe that every word of God is true.
No word of God is without power to be
Fulfilled just of itself if we believe.

In Proverbs 4 belief is shown to be
A discipline to work effectively.
In twenty through to twenty-two are verbs
That each can help submit one to God's word.

Attend, incline, let not depart and keep
God's word and all His benefits you'll reap.
God's medicine is ready to receive
For all who take the time to now believe.

63 *Wait on the Lord*

The most difficult thing for a Christian to do is to wait
On the Lord. But the ones who develop this skill receive great
Supernatural benefits. In Psalm One Hundred and Three,
Verses one through to twelve give a wonderful message indeed.

David tells himself in the first verse, "Bless the Lord, O my soul…"
He is praising the Lord. David's state of mind should be our goal.
For his level of fellowship with the Lord was unexcelled.
In this psalm he describes our New Covenant righteousness well.

For verse twelve says as far as the east does remain from the west
(That's incalculable. Travel east and you'll never hit west.),
That is how far the Lord has removed our iniquities from
Us. So David saw one day our righteousness would indeed come.

David learned the invaluable secret that few do embrace.
Seek the Lord with persistence and He will reward you with grace.
Years he spent tending sheep in the fields, talking to the Lord. He
Does describe his reliance on God's grace in Psalm Twenty-Three.

He that dwells in the secret place of the most High shall abide
'Neath the shadow of Almighty God. Can't beat that if you tried.
It just doesn't get better than this. He's our Father. His love,
As described in Psalm 91, shows us we're blessed from above.

64 *Faithful Abraham*

What is Faith? It's the substance of things that are hoped
For; the evidence of things not seen. It's the scope
Of our knowledge of God, knowing we are His loved
Ones and trust we that He holds our future above.

It's in Hebrews 11 that faith is explained.
These great men of the Bible through faith had obtained
Good reports. And by trusting in God they received
What He promised. Rewarded He them who believed.

Faithful Abraham, he's the man God used to start
A great nation of His chosen people. "Depart,"
He told Abraham, from his own kindred and dwell
In the land of the Canaanites, where he did well.

God assured Abraham from his own seed he would
Be the father of many; so many they could
Not be counted. And even though he was past age,
He believed in God's word, and his faith set the stage.

So in Genesis 12 this great story began.
What's amazing is knowing just how it was planned.
Generations of faithful men God did work through
To fulfill His great purpose that He pointed to.

From the very beginning God planned to reclaim
Us, His children through Jesus, our Saviour. His name
Is Redeemer; our Substitute. His blood He shed
For us all makes our spirits alive that were dead.

A most striking comparison Abraham makes
To our Father in Heaven. God asked him to take
His son Isaac to give as a burnt sacrifice.
And obeyed Abraham, trusting God would provide.

He bid Isaac to carry the wood that would be
Used on him, just like Jesus who carried the tree
He was crucified on. And as Abraham, he
Was prepared to slay Isaac, the Lord set him free.

God commended then Abraham, for he did not
Try to keep his one promised son Isaac from God.
For God later would offer up His only Son
Jesus Christ as our Sacrifice. His will be done.

This brave story is found chapter 22 in
The book Genesis. Hebrews 11 again
Paul retells it. In verses thirteen through sixteen
Paul tells how the faith of these great men could be seen.

For they had the desire for more than this short
Earthly life. They desired a country, the sort
That's in Heaven. A Heavenly city is where
God has made us a place, so believe if you dare.

65 Bible Translations

The most accurate Bible translation by far is King James.
And yet it is not perfect. Some questionable wording remains.
There are three scripture verses important, which do not live up
To original Greek. These are vital. Right here we'll discuss.

Fifty-three and verse four in Isaiah, it says "He hath borne
(All) our *griefs*, and (He) carried our *sorrows*." These words take a form
Not compatible with other times they are used. The word for
Grief is "makob." In Job this meant "**pain**" when they used it before.

Look and see for yourself, in Job 33:19 it's "pain."
Also *sorrows*, translated from "choli," the meaning is plain.
Every time it was used elsewhere in the Old Testament, the
Word for "choli" was "**sickness**." Isaiah just doesn't agree.

So this verse, it should say, "He hath borne (all) our **pains**…" (also He)
Carried (all of) our **sicknesses**." Now it makes sense. Also we
Have a backup. In Matthew 8:16 and 17 see
That by taking our sicknesses, Jesus fulfilled prophecy.

Know that healing is meant for today. It is not just a mere
Circumstance of the Bible that Jesus did heal. It's for here
And right now. As our Substitute on the cross, His sacrifice
Means He bore all our sins *and* our sicknesses. He paid the price.

And His name is above *every* name, yes, of every disease;
Every pain, every mental disturbance or deficiency.
In Philippians 2:9 it says so. Accept this and see
How your life can be blessed with good health. It's God's will that
you be.

Now the second significant scripture that might help you if
It was worded correctly is Romans 10:17. This
Verse says "Faith comes by hearing, and hearing by the word of *God.*"
This mistake may surprise you. It sounds right, but really, it's not.

In the Greek, it says "Christos." That's Christ, not our Father above.
And so faith comes by hearing the word, not of God, but of Love.
Jesus Christ is the Person who loves all mankind. He's the One;
God's free gift. For God so loved the world that He gave us His Son.

So by "hearing" Old Testament words showing how God did deal
With grave sinners who did not obey Him, would not make one feel
Very safe or forgiven or loved by their Father above.
One must hear the New Testament words of the Lord and His love.

For through Christ we're forgiven. Once we accept Jesus, then we
Are redeemed to our Heavenly Father. We're righteous and free
From the Law and God's judgment and wrath. He's not mad anymore.
So have faith in the Lord Jesus Christ, and rejoice evermore.

Psalm 8:5 is the last we'll discuss. This verse says God made man
To be just slightly lower than *angels.* The translators can
Not have suffered the courage to write what this really said. The
Word for angels was "Elohim." That's one of God's names, indeed.

"What is man, that thou (God) are (thus) mindful of him?" It does say

In verse four. Well apparently God did create us that day
In His image, and though we're not mighty like God, we are still
Esteemed highly by Him. Our importance to God is a thrill.

For God loves us, and gave us His Son to redeem us to Him.
The whole Bible, it's all about Jesus. God's plan was to win,
Without cheating, restored fellowship with Creation. That's man.
Also women. To understand how much God loves us is grand.

66   *Faith in His Grace*

The whole New Testament can be summed up in these four words: "Faith in

His Grace." His grace we do receive, and faith is what we have within.
Now faith is your part. It's not God's. While Grace is His part. It's not yours.
It's Jesus' sacrifice that makes you righteous and to God restores.

For when God looks at you, He does not see your flaws. He only sees
The righteousness you gained when you accepted Jesus and believed.
The sacrifice that Jesus made on Calvary has satisfied
The wrath of God. He is not mad. His Son He sent. For you He died.

So do not cheat yourself. Do not degrade the blessed position you
Possess, for "As He is," right now, in heaven, "so are we…" It's true.
It says so in 1 John 4:17. In this world we are just
Like Jesus, as He is right now. That we are righteous we should trust.

Is Jesus sick? Does He have cancer? Is He mentally impaired?
Is He possessed with demons? Is His future bleak? Does He get scared?
If Jesus lives within your spirit (once you're saved), you're just like Him.
So let your spirit, where He lives, affect your mind and every limb.

So how can we convince ourselves we have the same potential as
The Lord Himself? The trick is to let Him renew our minds. He has
Already paved the way for us. Yes, our redemption's been achieved.
The only move that's left is ours. Believe in Him. His grace receive.

67 *Don't Miss Out*

Don't miss out on God's best for you. He wants to bless you. But the
Only catch to receiving His blessing is that you must be
Focused on His Son Jesus, and not on yourself; only Him.
If you focus on Jesus and not on yourself, you will win.

In Luke 10, verses thirty-eight through forty-two is the tale
About Martha and Mary and Jesus. This story avails
A most valuable lesson. These ladies had two different views
About what was important. If you were one, who would you choose?

For in verse thirty-nine Mary chose to sit at Jesus' feet
And be blessed by His word, while her sister called Martha did meet
Supposed needs of her guests as she served them and scurried about;
Much perturbed that her sister, not helping her, took this time out.

And not only did Martha blame Mary for being lax, but
Martha even blamed Jesus for causing distraction. So what
Was she thinking? It's obvious she was absorbed with what she
Wanted, missing what most would consider the ultimate dream.

Just imagine if we, knowing what we know now, had the chance
To just sit at the feet of our Lord. God in flesh. We would dance!
Martha had it all wrong in her focus. But Mary perceived
That she needed the Lord and He did not need her. She believed.

So then Jesus told Martha that Mary had chosen the good
That was needful, while Martha was troubled with things that she should
Not be troubled about. Jesus told Martha what Mary chose
As her focus He would not take from her, as Martha supposed.

Mary's focus on Jesus was life changing. Look what she did
In John 12 and verse three, how she honored the Lord, for not hid
From her was His importance. He honored her back when He said
In verse seven, her purpose was pure. (In six days He'd be dead.)

Now let's look at the others who wanted to honor the Lord
The same way, in the end of Luke 23 to 24.
Before Sabbath prepared they the ointments on Jesus they'd use.
But they found not His body; too late. And this chance they did lose.

Who do you choose to be? Are you Martha, or Mary? The best
That God offers is waiting for you. Enter into His rest,
As it says in 4:9 through 11 of Hebrews. Who do
You keep dear in your heart? If it's Jesus, to you He'll be true.

68 *Be Strong in Grace*

Paul does tell us in Timothy's Second epistle in two
And verse one to "be *strong* in the grace that's in Christ," so then who
Is thus "weak" in His grace? It's the ones who don't realize that He
Is them with for all time. He will never forsake us nor leave.

When you know that you know that you know that He's with you,
this does
Make you bold, for the God that did say "Let there Be…" and there
was
The whole universe, He knows the number of hairs on your head.
When you know that He's with you, and loves you then nothing
you'll dread.

What is Grace? It's the freeness of God's gift to us, and His name,
It is Jesus, for Grace is a Person, Whose love we don't gain
By our efforts. His love is a blessing that we cannot earn.
Just accept divine favour from Jesus. His ways of grace learn.

We must know we are sanctified. Second Corinthians 5
Twenty-one, this explains why we're righteous and virtuous. Strive
To thus understand God made Him sin for us, Who knew no sin
So that "we might be made (then) the righteousness of God in Him."

So whenever you're troubled with doubt, then just hold your hands high
To the Lord and declare that you're righteous through Him. He is why
We are "innocent," yes, through the shed blood of Christ we're
redeemed
To our Father in Heaven. His children He highly esteems.

69 *Passion for Prayer*

Throughout His earth walk, Jesus was in touch, through prayer, with God above.

As much time as He spent with people, also He did pray. His love
For all mankind attracted souls. His God-intoxicated grace
Of endless fellowship with God did lure to Him the human race.

God works through prayers. Don't be deceived and not take seriously how
So very vital are your prayers. The angels' actions prayers allow.
First Thessalonians and five, verse seventeen tells us to pray,
And do not stop. It sounds impossible for us to pray this way.

But it is not impossible. One doesn't have to speak to pray.
Just be aware of Jesus. Think of Him. He'll guide you through your day.
And when you can devote some time, be still, and know that He is God;
Declares Psalm 46 verse ten. Of His peace none can you defraud.

Isaiah 40:31 says "they that wait upon the Lord …
Renew their strength;" Again, just think of Him. His peace is your reward.
He gives you strength to face your day, your week, your year; He's all you need.
Depend on Him throughout each day and absolutely you'll succeed.

70 *God Does Not Use Superstars*

Ecclesiastes 9:11 tells us how both time and chance
Are two strong factors in man's greatness. Much depends on
circumstance.
But there is yet another way one can achieve great status, though
It happens to those who don't seek to be somebody, don't you know.

When God's involved, the rules do change. They go from
meritocracy
(Which is the world's way, and it's good) to absolute humility.
In First Corinthians 1:26 to 31 we see
That God calls those who are not mighty, wise or noble naturally.

But God does choose the foolish to confound the wise, and also He
Confounds the mighty with the weak, and brings to nought the things
that be.
His way is thus. He does it this way so that no flesh glories in
His presence. Only Christ is just. Give Him the glory and you'll win.

What do we win? It tells us in verse thirty that through Christ we gain
Not only wisdom and redemption; righteousness do we attain.
We're sanctified; made holy by His sacrifice. Corinthians
The Second, 12 verse nine, it gives the key to our success in Him.

Rely on Jesus! Through our weakness He is strong. Don't think too much.

Don't try to solve it. Let Him have it. Don't you think He has the touch?

The God who spoke the universe into existence, He will use

You if you're humble. You will like the outcome when His grace you choose.

71 *Everyone Matters*

The red cherry tomatoes are ripe in the garden almost
All at once. Though there are many more that will ripen, the host
Of them were picked today. What to do with them? Share them. For the
Rest will be red and ready in days. A dilemma that's sweet.

As some dropped while I picked them, I couldn't help thinking that each
One's important. They must be included. I stooped down to reach
Them. A vision came into my mind, how this crop was just like
All the people on Earth. Empathy overwhelming did strike.

There's too many. Yet God knows the number of hairs on each head.
Whereas I can touch only a few lives each day, God instead
Knows exactly what everyone thinks, prays and needs; what they say
And their actions. All knowing. God's greatness just blows me away.

I accept that my mind is just tiny compared to my Lord.
He won't give me more than I can handle. But I have matured
In His grace. And the ones that are ripe to receive Him, if He
Sends them my way, He'll give me the right things to say to them, see.

It's so easy. All I have to do is be ready; aware
Of each person around me. His love fills my heart and I care
About others. But I am not perfect. I do still get tired;
Even grumpy. But Jesus forgives me and gets me inspired.

The old lady who sat in the restaurant eating alone
Looked so sad. I did pray asking Jesus to bless her. Unknown
Was she to me. While working, all that I could do was be kind
To her as she departed. His love I do pray that she'll find.

It's not my job to worry 'bout God's job. He doesn't need me.
But He does want to use me whenever I'm willing to be
Used by Him to help others. To grow in His grace is to know
Absolutely that everyone matters. His love tells me so.

72 *Through Him*

Ephesians 2:18 says, "For through Him we both have access (to
Our Father, God in Heaven) by one Spirit..." Understand that through
His sacrifice, our spirits now are joined to Him. Forever we
Are able to rely on God's great wisdom for eternity.

In John 16 we see Ephesians 2:18 now in reverse.
Verse thirteen through to fifteen Jesus tells us how God will converse
With us. This conversation will be through the Holy Spirit who
Will show things to our spirits; whatsoever Jesus tells Him to.

This sounds confusing, but it's not. The only way that you will know
What wisdom is available to you from God, He will bestow
To you through God the Holy Spirit. You must let your mind retrieve
This wisdom that's from God through your own spirit. That's how you
receive.

How do you get your mind to do this? Think on things above to win.
Don't be absorbed with life's affairs. Devote some mental time to Him.
The best way that I know to do this is to pray in tongues. You'll gain
His peace and love and wisdom, and your weaknesses will not remain.

Let's look at the example of King Solomon. In First Kings Three,
Verse five, God said to ask Him what he wants, appearing in a dream.
Verse nine and ten show Solomon did ask for wisdom, and this pleased
The Lord. The next three verses show God gave him that and more.
Indeed.

Immediately Solomon displayed the wisdom he had gained.
Verse sixteen to the end of chapter three reveal the story famed.
Two women quarreled over who was mother of a baby. One
Did steal the others' baby when her own child died. And this was
done

At night without a witness. Solomon proposed the child divide
In two, and give each woman half. The mother real did then decide
To give the baby up, so that her child would live. And then he knew
To give the baby to this woman, for she was the mother true.

The first ten chapters Solomon composed in Proverbs are about
This wisdom. Proverbs 4 verse seven indicates, there is no doubt,
That "Wisdom is the principal (or most important) thing." Verse
eight
And nine show by exalting Her you'll gain a crown of glory great.

73 *Three Conditions*

In Romans 6:14 Paul makes a most astounding statement. He
Informs us sin has no dominion over us, for we are free
From Law. We are not under law, but under grace. Though we must
choose
What to be governed by. One can miss out on grace and blessings lose.

Verse sixteen says that we are servants to the thing that we obey.
Choose grace, or law, or self. These are the three conditions of today.
It matters where we place our focus. Are you legalistic, or
Do you think mostly of yourself? Or do you think about the Lord?

So much can be observed within Paul's letters to two churches. These
Are the Corinthians and the Galatians. Notice Paul was pleased
With the Corinthians, despite how very carnal they had been.
In First Corinthians and three Paul fed them "milk," for they did sin.

But in Corinthians the First and chapter one, Paul called them "saints."
For they did fellowship with Jesus Christ, and they were under grace.
As long as one believes that they are righteous, all because of Him,
And not because of their own efforts, they can grow, in spite of sins.

In verse 1:8 Paul called them "blameless," to the end. You see, it's not
By their own effort that they were considered righteous. This they got
From Jesus. He's the only way that one can ever truly be
Made sanctified and "good enough" for Father God eternally.

But some do make the same mistake that the Galatians made. They try
To be accepted by their own good works or deeds, and so deny
That only by the grace of Jesus they are righteous. Chapter five
Verse one through eighteen show of Jesus' grace they did themselves deprive.

And in verse four Paul says that they are "fallen from (His) grace." And so
"Christ is become of no effect." By their own efforts they can't grow
In Christ. This legalism is the same as bondage. We are free
From Ten Commandments. Jesus puts His laws into our hearts you see.

So either Jesus paid it all, or He did not. Make up your mind.
Receive His gift of grace within your heart, or you will fall behind
By thinking that your own self-righteousness will get you where you need
To be. Do not be foolish thinking by your efforts you'll succeed.

This does work in the natural. Within this world, if you want to
Do better for your family and get ahead, your efforts do
Help get you there, with education and hard work. But do not let
This carry over to your fellowship with God. You might regret.

Depend on Him. He knows your needs much better than you'll ever know
Them by yourself. So trust in Him. He'll nudge you which way you should go.

He'll guide you in your choices. You won't make mistakes that cost
you. When
You face decisions, pray, and He will give you the right answers then.

The third condition one can have is when their consciousness revolves
Around themselves. They're self-absorbed. They do believe, but don't
resolve
To trust in God. In Revelation 3:16 and 17
The Lord describes this as "lukewarm," and He is not impressed with
these.

Just ask yourself, are you so confident or stubborn that you do
Not need the One who spoke the universe into existence; who
Created you? What makes you think that you can make it on your
own,
When all you have to do is seek Him. He will help you from the
throne.

Things happen that you can't control. But God knows everything.
So be
Aware of Him, His awesomeness, and trust Him for your every need.
I've said enough. The choice is yours. Says Romans 6, verse twenty-
two,
We're blessed with everlasting life when God is Who we're servants to.

74 *Successful Prayer*

Five steps there are to prayer that is successful. When we pray
The first thing we must know is this: the will of God. The way
We can be sure is when we find two scripture verses to
Back up our prayer, that it's God's will. Two verses. This will do.

A verse fantastic that does show God's will is 3 John 2.
This verse says that "above all things," the greatest are these two;
"That thou may *prosper* and (that thou may) *be in health*." These are
The two best things that we all want. God knows what we desire.

And furthermore, He wants to give them to us. We can find
More verses that will back these up. But sometimes with our minds
We have to "fight." We cannot waiver. And that brings us to
The second step of prayer. What is the will of God for you?

So be decisive. You must *know* within your heart that this
Is God's will for you. Do not waiver. Double-mindedness
Makes one unstable, as it says in James 1:8. So be
Convinced that what you want is what you'll get eventually.

Don't pray yet. You're not ready, quite. The third step is that you
Should be attentive with your eyes and ears. Just think it through.
There must be a *conversion* in your thinking. "Plan B" should
Not even cross your mind. You must believe God's plan is good.

If you decide, with prayer, that you should see a doctor; fine.
There's nothing wrong with this. Pray that the Lord gives them divine
Instruction, and/or guides a surgeon's hands. If this is how
You can believe for healing, then be firm in your mind now.

But if you can believe for miracles or healing by
The Lord without a doctor, then don't think that you'll just try
It this way first, and if it doesn't work, then maybe go
The doctor route. Do not be tossed by symptoms to and fro.

You really must be confident that something in your mind
Did change, and now you have no fear to hold your ground. Just find
This moment that the light went on inside your head and hold
Onto it firmly. Trust the Lord. Be patient and be bold.

This brings us to the fourth step now: Believe. "Of course," you say.
But Mark 11:24 says do this when you pray.
Be confident. You must believe that you receive right when
You pray. So focus on your prayer and *see it*, there and then.

So now you're ready. Pray you may. But always duplicate
The first three steps as often as you think to pray. It's great
To get into this habit. This will help you to believe.
Step 4's the key. Right when you pray, believe that you receive.

Step 5 is probably the hardest step: to Stand. Yes, *stand*.
Just hold your ground. Sometimes the answer does take time. Demand
The confidence and patience from yourself that you may need.
No matter what the circumstances are, "you will succeed."

You must succeed. Believe you will. The devil, he will try
Discouragement and condemnation; get you to deny
Your righteousness. Don't let him win. Be patient. Once again,
Some prayers take *time*, depending what or who's involved, and when.

So be aware of him. The devil, he is real. See in
Ephesians, verse 6:12 and 13 warn you how to win;
To stand. In verses fourteen through to eighteen, they do tell
You how to stand against the devil. Prayer will serve you well.

The story that's in Second Chronicles and twenty may
Help you to stand. In verses ten to twelve show the dismay
Of Israelites. But God gives them the answer; verse fifteen.
They have God's word. The battle is not theirs, but His it seems.

So if they put their trust in God, He told them they'd succeed.
For He'd be with them. He's their only hope, and met their need.
So all of Judah and Jerusalem, they praised the Lord.
They worshipped Him and trusted Him that He would be their
sword.

Read to verse twenty-four and see how their attackers fell.
They wiped each other out; not one left standing. See as well
How they did leave behind great spoils of wealth. The Israelites,
Because they kept their eyes on Him, they didn't have to fight.

To pray successfully there is, on our part, a response
To grace required. Prayer is a skill that we develop. Once
We have success, our confidence will grow, and we will see
That life is so much nicer when His grace abounds our needs.

75 *Why Tongues*

When one asks, "Why should I pray in tongues?" two more
questions arise.
"Why is this so important to me?" is the first. And surprised
You may be by the answers. But also, "Why did Jesus not
Pray in tongues?" What a curious question. The answer we've got.

It all started in Acts chapter two. Pentecost was the day
When one hundred and twenty had gathered together to pray.
Verses one through eleven, the story amazing they tell
How they all spoke with tongues that the other Jews recognized well.

The new Church, it was born on this day. The beginning of our
Dispensation, the church age, continues, where God gives us power
By His Spirit, the Holy Ghost. Once you receive Him, you gain
A prayer language of your very own. Your flaws need not remain.

First Corinthians 14 verse two shows us clearly, to pray
In the Spirit is praying in tongues. God, He gave us this way
To communicate with Him. You're speaking to God; not to men.
And verse four shows this edifies *you*. You will benefit then.

It's a mystery, what we tell God through the Spirit. And we
Truly don't know what things we are praying. The purpose you see
Is to bypass your mind, which is limited. You know your thoughts
Can be carnal. You don't always know what to pray as you ought.

And so edification's the key. This will change you; your mind.
You won't notice the change right away in your thinking. You'll find
Though that clearly your thoughts, they have changed. Any grudges you had;
Any hang-ups or selfishness, these changed to good thoughts from bad.

Now the devil, he does not appreciate this kind of prayer.
For like you, he cannot understand it. But he is aware
That this prayer, it will help you. He doesn't want that. So he will
Try his best to deter you and cause you to think tongues are "ill."

"Tongues are not for today," or "You need an interpreter to
Pray in tongues." No you don't. That's a myth. Tongues develop in you
A like-mindedness to Jesus Christ. Tongues remove selfishness
As it says in Philippians 2:4 and 5. You He'll bless.

This is why, Jesus, He never needed to pray in tongues. He
Was the same in His mind as He was in His Spirit. To be
In a fellowship constant with Father, that's how Jesus lived
His life daily. His mind was as pure as His Spirit could give.

And we have Him; Who Jesus had. He had the Holy Ghost. See
In Acts 10:44 and the next verse, plus forty-six, we
All receive Him, each one of us. No one's left out. Magnify
Him is what we will do with our tongues, and we won't even try.

Magnify Him. Yes, He'll become bigger to you in your mind.
Not that He changed, but *you* did. And you will now have a new kind

Of encounter with Father and Jesus. You'll see them anew.
Again, they didn't change; only you did. Embrace the new you.

How exciting it is when you realize the cobwebs are gone
From your mind. They've been swept away clean and you will not
miss one.
Romans 8:26, it explains this phenomena. Strange
How unknown is this prayer that took four thousand years to arrange.

76 *Prayer and Evangelism*

The prayer of importunity is when you pray for others. Look
At these examples in the Bible of this prayer. Within the book
Of Romans 1, verse seven through to nine, it tells us we should pray
Incessantly for others, and to mention them in prayers each day.

And also in Colossians 1, verse three and nine, Paul once again
Encourages this constant prayer for others. When you pray for men
And women, always think about the process that must be achieved.
The subject of your prayer may not be ready. They may not receive.

And that is why, to pray for others, you must be relentless. They
May cancel out your prayer with negativity. The words they say
Do matter. So you do not know how many times you must repeat
A prayer for it to take effect; it may take years to be complete.

Now when you pray for you, to pray successfully, you do not need
Vain repetitions. Pray it once and then have faith that you'll succeed.
But when you pray for others, that is when you need persistence.
When
You intercede for others you are standing in the gap for them.

This type of prayer is so important. Intercession sometimes is
The only chance that some may have. Divine protection lets them
live.
In Luke 13's where Jesus clearly taught this concept. Will you be
Someone who prays for those who do not take salvation seriously?

Imperative it is to also pray for the unsaved, and in
Most cases prayer that works for Christians also works for them. To win
Lost souls, a verse effective's in Corinthians the Second. From
5:17 to 21 explains how far, through Christ, we've come.

For these five verses make the gospel captivating. First they show
The newness that we gain through Christ. Old things are passed away, and those
Old ugly feelings, they will be wiped out. No effort on your part
Required. Receive is all one needs to do to have a brand new start.

For few will want to be a Christian if they're told that first they must
Confess their sins or give them up. That's not what Jesus said. One just
Asks Jesus to become their Saviour. He will do the rest. Yes He
Puts His laws, love and faith, into our hearts. And so from works we're free.

As Peter tells us in the First of his epistles, 3:15;
At all times ready we should be to tell an asker what it means
To be in Christ; the reason for the hope that's in us. There's a need
For Laborers to spread the news of Jesus and to plant the seeds.

So back to intercession. When we pray for others, here is how
Our prayers get answered. If they're Christians, then the Holy Spirit now
Is in them, in their spirit. He can talk directly to their mind
From deep inside. Divine advice within; the Holy Spirit kind.

Or Angels, they can be dispatched to "talk" to someone from without.

They'll make suggestions to ones' mind. Good thoughts. But also have no doubt

That this is how the devil works. He also makes suggestions to

Our minds, and tries deceiving us. So weigh your thoughts and think them through.

The third way is when Laborers, that's other people, Christians, they

Get "sent" to talk to someone when they get a "nudge." If they obey

This nudge, then they may truly help the one that you've been praying for.

We're all included in this "job" description, so obey the Lord.

Thank you Jesus.

77 *The First Evangelist*

When Jesus sat alone at Jacob's well in chapter 4 of John,
He knew He'd have a visitor while His disciples they had gone
To purchase meat. Verse four says that "He must needs go…" this way, for He
Kept His "divine appointment" with a woman there he had to see.

The woman of Samaria did not expect to see Him there
At Jacob's well. She went when it was hot, avoiding those she dared
Not mingle with. She had a reputation. For the man that she
Was with was not her spouse; five husbands she'd already had.
Indeed.

It does make sense to think she was avoiding other women who
Would criticize and make her feel like dirt. Did Jesus taunt her too?
Of course He didn't. And in fact, He complimented her when she
Told Him the truth about her life. He treated her with dignity.

The Lord does not condemn. That's what the world does. Jesus, He
is not
Like men. He's God in Man. He was the first, since the "first Adam."
What
Most people do not understand is God is Love. And Jesus came
To earth as God in flesh, to show us humbly, we can be the same.

Yes, we can be the same as Him. That's why he told the woman in
Verse ten that if she knew the gift of God, and who He was, well then

She could have asked, and He would give her living water.
Furthermore,

She'd never thirst again, for "everlasting life" is what's in store.

She talked of the Messiah, and then Jesus told her, "I that speak
(To) thee am He." So on that day her status grew to be unique.

For she, a woman, is the very first to whom Lord Jesus told

He is the Christ. And from then on transformed she was from meek
to bold.

She is the first evangelist. She instantly obeyed her call.

She went to town and told the men, "Come, see a man, which told
me all

Things that I ever did: is not (then) this the Christ?" The men
believed

In Him, and all because of her strong testimony they'd received.

78 *Wonders of Worship*

The sweet Psalmist of Israel, David, he understood how
Praise and worship would bless him. Just like it did then, it will now.
In Psalm 34:7 it says the Lord camps round about
Those that fear Him. Delivers He them from distress. Have no doubt.

Now to "fear" the Lord, that's just like worship; a form of respect.
Although He expects nothing, some gratitude can't hurt. In fact
It works wonders. His Grace is incredible, as David knew.
Let us look near the end of First Samuel to witness this truth.

In verse 21:10 David fled from King Saul who did seek
To destroy him, but he went to Gath where his chances were bleak,
For they recognized David who had slayed Goliath, so he
Then feigned madness, which worked, for King Achish then bade
him to leave.

In verse 22:1 and 2 David departed and he
Did escape to Adullam, a cave, where he had company.
All his brethren did join him, with others who were in distress.
They were down on their luck, discontented, and some were in debt.

So these 400 men were downtrodden, and David became
Their bold leader. Through time spent with him they were never the
same.
See how David, their captain, he chose not to wallow in grief.
Circumstances were bad, but he would not accept a defeat.

And in Psalm 34:1 through 7, which David wrote when
He had made this escape to this cave shows his attitude then.
In verse three he encouraged the others to worship the Lord,
And verse five shows this lifted their spirits; shame felt they no more.

So you see how he faced this grave challenge; with praise! David chose
Not to claim a defeat for himself and the others. He rose
Above dire circumstances, for he knew the value of trust
In the Lord. This example repeated by all is a must.

Well, it's only a must if you want to be blessed. We all do
Face harsh challenges. No one escapes them. Admit this is true.
But prepared we can be just like David. His habit was praise.
So when hardship did strike, he could handle it. Blessed were his days.

Can you further imagine if David had been able to
Pray in tongues? He was born much too early. Yet somehow he knew
About Grace. He knew one day our sins, far removed they would be
From us, as he said in verse twelve of Psalm One Hundred and Three.

So remember, whenever there's trouble, just worship the Lord.
This may not change the details but this will change you. And restored
To you will be His peace and His joy. Just like David, you'll be
One who knows what to do when the going gets tough. You will see.

79 *The Book Before The Book*

Jesus tells us in Luke chapter ten and verse twenty, "Rejoice,"
For our names are all written in heaven, all who made the choice
To receive Him. And so it would seem there prevails a great book
That existed before all of us. In the Bible we'll look.

In Psalm 139 we're shown how much God knows all about
Every one of His children. He knows every thought; every doubt.
We are fearfully, wondrously made. Verse sixteen states each one
Of our members in His book were written, when yet there was none.

In Ephesians 1:4 and 1:5 we are given a glance
That God not only knew us; He chose us. We're not His by chance.
He chose who would believe in the Lord and accept Him by grace.
Through His blood all our sins were forgiven before they took place.

Revelation's near end; 21:27 first names
This great book as the Lamb's Book of Life, which includes all who
claim
Dear Lord Jesus as Saviour, Messiah, Redeemer, God's gift
Freely given. Delivered He us from the curse He did lift.

This great mystery that we were known long before we were born;
Every detail of who we are now not obscured from the One
Who created us, it's inexplicable; hard to perceive.
It's by faith we accept God's pure love and in Jesus believe.

80 *When I Die*

I'm not afraid of death; not anymore. So close we are to the
Eternal side of life, when from this earthly body we are free.
How frail we truly are. Not much it takes to stop a beating heart.
It's by the grace of God that we are here each day. Let's make a start.

Let's make a start to live each day for Jesus, for through Him we can
Have fellowship with God our Father. Jesus makes us righteous.
Then
For those of us who are not ready to depart, the Lord, He will
Set angels of protection 'round us, plus the ones we pray for still.

Amazingly some live through accidents that should have killed them,
while
Some others do not make it. What's the difference? I can tell you.
Smile,
Because your Father loves you, and when you accept His free gift,
you
Are now redeemed to Him. He will protect you, and your loved ones
too.

Psalm 91 verse one says "He that dwelleth in the secret place
Of the most High (he) shall abide (beneath) the shadow of (His
grace,)
Almighty (God)." Just ponder on this verse. If you're not blown away
By what it says, you need to pinch yourself. Our God, He lives today.

The living God redeemed us to Himself by the Lord Jesus. He's
Our Saviour. By accepting Him's the only way that we can be
Made holy, righteous, "good enough" for God our Father. Through
His love
We now are "heirs," or children of the most High God. Seek Him
above.

Colossians 3 verse one says "...Seek those things which are above...,"
for we
Are "dead." Our lives are "hid with Christ in God." It says so in verse
three.
Yet many people on this earth store up their wealth, in fear, or greed.
But we that dwell beneath His shadow trust that He supplies our needs.

First Peter 1, verse twenty-two through twenty-five explains it all.
Our souls are purified when through the Spirit we obey our call.
The Lord wants us to love each other with a love that's pure, which
He
Put in our hearts when we accepted Him, and "born again" are we.

Our lives are but a whisper, or a blade of grass. And when we're in
Our prime, well this is like the flower of that grass; so brief. Again,
Does Peter thus remind us, Jesus' word endures forever. We
Are taught this through the gospel. We will live for all eternity.

So all the world's injustice, and unfairness, though disturbing, does
Not weigh much in the long run when compared to life eternal. Was
The price that Jesus paid upon the cross enough to satisfy
The wrath of God? It was. His substitution paid our debt so high.

So Mom and Dad, I'll see you soon. But please Lord, not just yet. You see,

I know within my heart I still have purpose on this earth, to be

Someone who blesses others, leading them to Christ. Plus I have strong

Desire to see my daughter grow in Jesus' love her whole life long.

But I will die, and when I do, I know that I will be in awe

Of all the wonders God has waiting for me. And this hope I draw

From stories I believe, of those who went to Heaven and returned

To earth to share mere glimpses, indescribable, of what they learned.

And also, in Corinthians the First, 2:9 Paul tells us we

Have neither seen nor heard, nor have our hearts conceived the things which He,

God has prepared for us that love Him. Heaven, this must be what Paul's

Describing. If we knew for sure how good it is, who'd wait at all?

81 *Portrait of Jesus*

Let me tell you the story of how I was so very blessed
By the lives of two innocent children. Now who could have guessed
That their visits to heaven could have such an impact on me,
And well, everyone. Why God used children is easy to see.

Let us start with young Colton. His story's amazing. If you
Haven't read it, or seen it, like I hadn't, well, you should do
Your own self a big favor. Read 'Heaven's for Real.' Then you'll know
Irrefutably, Heaven's for real. A young boy tells us so.

In the movie edition of young Colton's novel there are
A few pictures, including a portrait of Jesus. By far
Is this likeness unique. It was painted by child prodigy
Akiane when she was just eight. Brave is her modesty.

She gives credit to God for her talent. She knows in her heart
That this gift she must share with all others. She's doing her part.
What's exciting's that Colton confirmed, "This is Jesus!" And so
Is this likeness of Jesus an accurate one. Good to know.

For I now have a picture of Jesus that's clear in my mind.
I believe Jesus wanted to bless me this way. He is kind.
Let me backtrack to how the Lord showed this to me. This is not
An ordeal I would want to repeat. I sure worried a lot.

Pastor Jack, he has told us repeatedly, many times, "Don't
Concentrate on your troubles. Just focus on Jesus. He won't
Let you down." Well, I finally listened. Consumed with much fear
I did sketch with a pen on a sticky note Jesus' face here.

And amazingly, staring at Jesus, it made me forget
All my fears. I was able to work without anguish. I let
His peace cover my mind. But this story gets better. Along
Came this book in my hands, and my impulse to read it was strong.

So I copied His portrait and taped it right next to the one
That I sketched at my job. It occurred to me, Jesus, God's Son
Wanted me, insignificant me, to know Him; see His face.
How exciting. But not only me; the entire human race.

Thank you Jesus for using two children who were not yet old
Enough to let the world motivate them. Their stories so bold.
Thank you Jesus that we now can see You, for real. This is You.
I believe it. And oh how I'm blessed by your portrait that's true.

82 *Make a Mark for Mark*

"How senseless. What a waste," is all your heart can think because the one
You love is gone. They took their life. No going back. Can't be undone.
You might have had some suicidal thoughts yourself. Don't let them stay.
They're false, demonic. Seek the Lord. You can wake up to brighter days.

Mark Kaylor was a high school senior, full of fun and kindness. He
Was facing something no one knew was troubling him to that degree.
He left behind a mother and big sister who'd give anything
To change that day. They'd talk to him about it; maybe dull the sting.

This desperation comes from Satan. He delights in causing pain.
Not only does he lead his victim to their death, the pain he gains
Of victims loved ones. They hurt too, immensely. Only time will heal
This gaping wound. The devil doesn't care if you don't think he's real.

If you don't think he's real, then that much easier he can deceive
You. He'll suggest an ugly thought right to your mind, and you'll believe
It came from you. He'll watch how you react to harmful thoughts he gave
You, for he cannot read your mind. And then he'll know what made you cave.

The Lord is your protection. He has given you His word. It's in
The Bible. Yes, it's all about the battle in your mind. Within
The living Bible, you will find His words of life. He gave us all
We need to live successfully. And on your life He's placed a call.

Not only does He want you to succeed, He wants you to impart
To others what you've learned. There is so much to know. Let's
make a start.
Philippians 4:8, it tells you how to train your mind to have
Good thoughts. It's so important to have healthy thoughts you
changed from bad.

What do you gain by training how you think? Philippians 4:9
Does tell you if you follow Him, you gain His peace. You'll have
divine
Protection and assistance, and yes, guidance. You'll know what to do
When faced with situations or hard choices. He will mentor you.

But you must give your time to Him. Devote some time. That's what
it takes.
Allow Him to renew your mind. Then you'll avoid some grave
mistakes
You could have made. Your mind He'll fill with peace. Through your
example He
Can show all others, "This is how to live, and let your mind be free."

So many people hurt, like Mark. It doesn't have to be this way.
God loves you, and that's why He sent His Son to take your place
that day.
If this does not make sense to you, it will. Seek Him above and you
Will understand the reason you exist, and things eternal too.

83 *You Are What You Think*

Proverbs 23:7 says "…as (someone) thinks in his heart,
So is he…" So you are what you think. You do play a big part
In the path your feet follow. Whose guidance do you listen to?
Is it God, or the world, or yourself? Who's important to you?

Is your glass now half full, or half empty? This does say a lot
About how you do see things in life. Negativity's not
Something that will lead one to success. Your success you can thwart
By the way that you think, and expressly on whom you resort.

If you're satisfied with the direction you're headed, then keep
Thinking how you already think. But if it's change that you seek,
Then you must change your thought life. It's you who must do it. No
one
Else can change how you think but yourself. Well, except for God's
Son.

Yes, the Bible can help you. From Acts chapter two 'til the end;
The New Testament covers the grace we are governed by. Then
The Old Testament does contain books most essential that do
Not pertain to the Law; Ten Commandments. These are helpful too.

They include Psalms and Proverbs, and Job, plus Isaiah, for most
Of it prophesies of the New Testament. The Holy Ghost,
He will teach you of Jesus, for He is your key to success.
The more knowledge of Him that you have, the more you He can
bless.

Recognize though that reading Old Testament books provides great
Understanding of how far we've come as God's children. Relate
To these less privileged people, and learn from mistakes that they made.
And be thankful to Jesus. Our sins God already forgave.

Nearly everyone probably has an agenda that does
Not match yours. Your best interest is not in their heart. And because
There's a devil out there, be aware of him. You should not let
Down your guard. Trust the Lord; only Him. No surprises you'll get.

Seek enlightenment. Paul says in 1:17 and 18
Of Ephesians that God gives us wisdom that only is seen
Through the knowledge of Jesus. So get revelation of Him.
It's more valuable than purest gold. He will bless you to win.

So to follow the world's way might lead to success, but you take
Certain risks, and you might not have peace. Trust the Lord. For you make
Your way prosper by knowing His word. In Philippians 2
And verse five says the way Jesus thought, "Let this mind be in you…"

84 *Heart of the Children*

Will there be one more like John the Baptist before the return
Of the Lord Jesus Christ? From two prophesies we can discern
John the Baptist did half of the prophecy. Malachi 4
And verse six, when compared to Luke 1:17 shows there's more.

In Luke 1's where we learn Zacharias, John's father was told
By the angel that he'd have a son who'd be guilelessly bold,
Like Elijah. He'd turn hearts of fathers to children, and he
Would make ready a people prepared for the Lord, he decreed.

Many Biblical scholars believe there will be one more "John"
To precede the return of the Lord. And this thought is based on
Verse 4:6, where not only will hearts of the fathers be turned
To the children. The children will honor their dads in return.

If we look at the world of today, we can see this is true.
Most kids, even when raised in a strong Christian family do
Oft' abandon their faith for a time. But sometimes they come back
When they realize life's hard without Jesus. His guidance they lacked.

And of course some completely forsake what they learned in their
youth.
This is sad. What disaster will they have to face 'til the truth
Of the cross brings them back? If they're lucky, they have someone
who
Loves and prays for them; stands in the gap. And that's all we can do.

So if I live to see it, I'll watch for the man who is sent
To the world to warn all of us, "Watch for the Lord and repent."
But I won't see who makes it. That trumpet will blow and then I
Will be gone from this earth to be caught up with Christ in the sky.

85 Growing Up

God knows that we all need to grow up first before He can
Begin to use us. He knows when we're ready for His plan.
It seems the troubles that we face as we grow up are ways
The Lord gets our attention. We wake up to brighter days.

Most young adults, they want their chance to have some fun; to fall
In love, or just get rowdy, reckless, drunk. When alcohol's
Involved, the lure is strong. Some never do recover from
This lust. But most mature and more responsible become.

But God will not use those who think that they're above the rest.
They think that they're entitled; narrow-minded; self-obsessed.
But they get old. We all do. Someone steps into their place.
And if they gain some wisdom, things above they might embrace.

Let's look at Moses, whom God used in Exodus. He was
A prime example of the type of man God uses. Does
It make much sense, when he was in his prime at 40, he
Was not near ready, and to Midian he then did flee.

In Exodus and chapter three is when the Lord stepped in
To Moses' life. He now was 80; nothing like he'd been.
No confidence did he have now. No pride; just humble. He
Was even reassured by God, that with him He would be.

The great days, they don't last. Time marches on. And time it takes
To understand what once we thought important's been replaced
By simpler things in life. Now we appreciate the good
Things that the Lord has blessed us with. We thank Him like we
should.

86 *God Wants to be Known*

How do most people go through life without awareness of
Their Father who created them, in Heaven up above.
They know of Him, but He's not on their minds. Most of their time
In thought is squandered on themselves, to reason without rhyme.

For there's no rhyme when one can see the world's amazing sights
And not attribute them to God. They're blind without the light
Of Jesus permeating every thought. His wisdom brings
A sense of awe to life on earth and touches everything.

Now let's go back in history, way back, before the men
Of earth knew God. How did He make His presence known? Back
then
The God of Abraham, of Isaac, and of Jacob, He
Connected with a few select who knew His Sovereignty.

Job understood the mightiness of God. In verses five
Through fourteen of Job 37 God's might is described.
In verse thirteen and fourteen we are told God's ways are known
To none. Be still, and know that He is God. He's on the throne.

In Exodus, when God set free His chosen people, He
Destroyed a nation, just to show the world His Majesty.
He didn't have to do it this way. Parting the Red Sea,
And all the other miracles gave credibility.

Don't mess with God's elect, the Israelites. This is the theme
Repeated all throughout the Testament of Old it seems.
But then we come to Jesus in the New, and now we see
That God wants ALL to be redeemed to Him. From death we're
free.

So understand that God went to a lot of trouble to
Make all of us aware of Him, plus all that He will do
And has already done for us. Your Father loves you so
Much; more than you can possibly imagine. Good to know.

87 *The Power of Your Words*

There's power in the spoken word. So be
Aware of what you say. Don't think you're free
To just say anything you want without
A consequence. That words have life don't doubt.

Know "Death and life are in the power of
The tongue..." says Proverbs 18:21.
So by your words you shall be justified,
Or by them be condemned. Words matter. Why?

In Matthew 12 does Jesus say that you
Are like a tree that's known by what it's fruit
Is like. Do you give good or bad fruit? See,
Your heart's your mind, and from it you will speak.

In Matthew 15 Jesus taught what goes
Into the mouth does not defile one. Know
You not that what comes out is what can cause
One harm? Before you speak, first think or pause.

In James 3:4 through verse 3:6 we see
There's power in the tongue. How can it be
So small and yet so powerful? Control
Your tongue, and thus keep trouble from your soul.

Sometimes you make it very easy for
The devil to deceive you. Know that your
Words spoken tell us what goes on inside
Your mind. Your thoughts in words you cannot hide.

Most people are not worth the devil's time
Or effort. Words and deeds reflect their mind's
Condition. Just as long as they don't talk
Of Jesus or His grace, he'll let them walk.

The Israelites in Numbers 14 shows
They got just what they spoke. They murmured so
By claiming God would let them die without
The Promised Land. They cursed themselves, no doubt.

When someone prayed for you to take that test
Successfully, the angels did their best
To help you. But you said, "I'm gonna fail."
Their hands were tied. This prayer your tongue derailed.

Or when you asked the Lord to heal you. Then
You felt the symptoms coming back again,
And waivered. You said, "I'm still sick. It's back."
You did not stand against this false attack.

Don't make predictions that are harmful to
Your own success, like "I can never do
This right." You "can't" because you said it. So
If you're not sure, just bite your tongue and go.

Yes, train your tongue. Don't let it "fly" without
A harness. That's your mind. Just think about
The words you say. They mean so much. And you
Can speak them to your benefit, so do.

88 *Repeat Teaching*

Don't get bored with the Biblical stories you know.
For you think you're an expert already. Not so.
There's so much we can learn we did not see before.
It's revealed to us little by little; no more.

For our spiritual growth is a process that does
Take significant time; our whole lives. And because
Knowledge does seep in slowly to brain cells, it's good
To repeat the essentials, to learn what we should.

Verse 3:4 through 3:7 of Titus explain
What through Jesus' incredible mercy we've gained.
Verse 3:8 does then tell us that we should affirm
These things constantly, so to maintain what we've learned.

Did you ever look back on years past in disgust
And think, "Oh how I'm glad I've matured." Well then trust
That you're not likely done. You still have so much more
To receive. Life's more peaceful as we do mature.

If you already "know" it, the next step is to
Be established. Let knowledge of Jesus take root.
This brings confidence. Then you will know that you know
God is Good! And He loves you. Thank Jesus it's so!

89 *The Cross*

It's not what men did, nailing Jesus to the cross that's so
Appalling. It was Father God who put Him there, you know.
"It pleased the Lord to bruise him" says Isaiah 53
Verse ten. Eleven says that God is "satisfied." Indeed.

God's satisfied? To understand, you need to see the whole
Grand story. In Isaiah 53's the purpose told
Of Jesus' death upon the cross. This "righteous servant" died
In substitution for our sins, and many justified.

Six thousand years ago, in Genesis it all began.
God knew that man would fall. Right from the start He had a plan;
To send to earth a Saviour, not from Adam's tainted seed.
We know that Jesus came from Mary; Holy Ghost conceived.

So Jesus bypassed Adam's flawed sin nature that he got
When he chose disobedience to God. This choice was not
A good one for mankind. All born of Adam (you and me)
Inherit still this curse. Our flesh has sin propensity.

Some fifteen hundred years before the cross did Moses bring
The Law. Man's inability to keep the law's a sting
To show us that we need a Saviour, Jesus. For without
His gift of righteousness, we fail. He's what it's all about.

We cannot be redeemed to Father God without Him. In
The Book of Romans, chapter eight, there's much to learn of sin.
God sending His own Son in likeness of our sinful flesh,
Condemned sin in the flesh so we could be His righteousness.

Let's look at what God did to Jesus on the cross. At first
It all seemed normal. With the others hanging He conversed.
But near the end God put on Jesus all the sickness, yes,
And sins of man; past, present, future. Jesus was a mess.

Isaiah 52:14 says that "his visage was
So marred (much) more than any man..." He was a blob. It does
Make sense to think the last He took was mental illness. How
Could He endure this very long? Thank God it's over now.

Yes, God is satisfied. Two thousand years ago His plan
For restoration and redemption of mankind began
When Jesus, His own Son became our humble servant. He
Did show us, "God is Love." Let's praise Him for eternity!

90 *Impossible*

It is clearly impossible for us to do what the Lord told us we
Ought to do in Luke 6:27 to 30. I'm sure you'll agree.
In these verses it says we're to love those who hate us; do good to
them. Yes,
Even pray for the ones who despitefully use us. When cursed we're to
bless.

If a person does smite your left cheek, you're to offer your right. And
to those
Who take anything from us, it says we're to let them take more. Well
suppose
That they actually ask; then accommodate. Furthermore, do not
expect
To get anything back. This completely erases one's own self-respect.

This is all about selflessness. Who then can do it? Not anyone I
Know, but Jesus. And that's just the point He was making, I'm sure.
We can try
To deceive ourselves, thinking we're "good enough." That's
something we'll never be
On our own. We need Him. He's our Substitute. Through Him we
have been redeemed.

Read Luke 6:31, the next verse. It says as you would have others do
Unto you, likewise do unto them. Matthew 7, verse twelve says this too.

This is the "Golden Rule." This is well known and famous. But now read the rest

Of verse twelve. This is "law," and we know all will fail at it; even the best.

All but Jesus that is. This is why He became for us "sin." In 8:3

Of Paul's book to the Romans it says "what the law could not do (for you see)

It was weak through the flesh, (so) God sending his Son in the likeness of (our)

Sinful flesh, and for sin, (did) condemn sin in (our sinful) flesh in that hour.

In that hour (more like six) when He hung on the cross, God judged sin in His Son.

And so now God's no longer concerned with our actions. His judgment is done.

All God sees is our state; state of "being," not sin. When we're "in Adam" we

Have no life in our spirit, but when we're "in Christ" we are righteous, indeed.

91 *The Best Prayer*

The best prayer you can pray for saints (believers) is Ephesians one.
It's all about enlightenment; a revelation of God's Son.
This prayer won't work for nonbelievers. They don't have God's life within
Their spirit. This is all about our righteousness. We're free from sin.

Some Christians need this prayer because they do not understand that they
Are righteous, not by anything they did themselves. The only way
Is Jesus. Only Jesus. It's God's goodness that will lead one to
Repentance, Romans 2:4 says, so see what Jesus did for you.

Verse seventeen says pray that God may give you knowledge of the Lord
By wisdom and by revelation through your spirit. Climb on board,
With open mind, this train of understanding and enlightenment,
Says verse eighteen, so that you'll know what benefits for you are meant.

Your mind must be enlightened. In Ephesians 4:18 Paul warns
That you can cut your mind off from the life of God when you do scorn
His wisdom, and your heart is hard. You're stubborn, and you think you know
It all already. There is nothing God can do to help you grow.

You still have God within your spirit. So you're saved. But that is all.
Your mind is dark. You have no power, all because you're thinking small.

What power? Verse nineteen informs us we have access to God's might,

For healing, peace, abundant blessings. In our spirit is God's Life.

The Holy Spirit who raised Jesus from the dead, He lives within
Your spirit. Romans 8:10 says, "...the body's dead because of sin;"
But know your spirit is alive because of righteousness. So who
Did you receive this from? It is of God. And you have been made new.

92 *Laser Beam*

Just like a laser beam of light does God direct His power. He
Can wipe out tumors, sickness, pain, mend broken bones; all instantly.
The catch is that you must believe He can, and will. Oh yes, He can.
For all the promises of God, through Jesus Christ, are yes/amen.

Paul says so in Corinthians the Second, verse 1:20. We
Can see a good example of God's pure directed energy
In John 18, verse three through six, when Judas brought the Pharisees
And men to capture Jesus in the Garden of Gethsemane.

When Jesus asked "Whom seek ye?" and they answered, "Jesus…,"
then He told
Them "I am He," and down they fell. Just them, and Judas with them.
Know
That only Father God could make the bad ones fall, all at the same
Time. Maybe God was showing them there's power when they use
that Name.

Sometimes these miracles don't happen instantly. You must believe
That Jesus made you righteous, and through Him alone, you will
receive
Your miracle of healing, wealth, whatever you are asking for.
Just find a verse to stand on, so if it's God's will you can be sure.

It IS God's will for you to prosper, and for you to be in health.
John says so in his third epistle, verse 1:2. Some think that wealth
Is not God's will, but He is not against it. When a saint is blessed
And "hears" Him, and obeys Him, they can help another who has
less.

Some even think that it's God's will for them to have an illness. Why
Would they then see a doctor to get better and God's will deny?
But if you want to know the truth, just read the Bible, pray and learn
God's wisdom and His will for you. Let Him renew your mind in
turn.

93 *Everywhere*

If God the Father, God the Son
And God the Holy Ghost are One,
Then true it is that He can be
Three places at one time you see.

But even more than this He can,
Because in every heart of man
Who trusts in Jesus, He abides.
Within our spirits He resides.

So one can see He's everywhere.
And for His church, us, He does care
So deeply that He did endure
The cross, the agony, the cure.

So God experienced our pains
And joys of life. This knowledge gained
He for the very purpose of
Redeeming us with His great love.

So when we say God gave His Son,
He gave Himself. His work is done.
All we must do is just believe,
And all His promises receive.

94   *The Spirit is Life*

The word "Trinity" you will not find in the Bible, but we
Know that God is three Persons; the Father and Jesus and the
Holy Ghost. 8:11 of Romans; one verse has all three.
In "the Spirit of Him that raised Jesus," the Trinity see.

Read the rest of this verse. It's exciting. It says that the Ghost,
Or the Spirit of Him that raised Jesus dwells IN us. The most
We can hope for, we have. God that raised Christ from death also will
"Quicken" our mortal bodies (that's Life) by His Spirit. A thrill.

It's a thrill to know God gave us life by His Spirit that dwells
Right within us. My spirit's alive. So is yours. Saved from hell.
But that's only the tip of the iceberg that hell we've escaped.
How abundant our lives can now be once we understand grace.

Romans 5:17 says much more they that choose to receive
An abundance of grace (righteousness!), for they choose to believe
In the Lord Jesus Christ, by His grace they shall reign in this life
With unmerited favor. His gift. No more anguish or strife.

And the "Zoe" of God, or the substance He's made of, well this
Is what's now in our spirit. His life. There is no better gift.
Chapter 1 of Ephesians explains we are all greatly blessed;
Highly favored, forgiven and loved. We are His righteousness.

95 *Chastisement*

Let me ask you a question. Are you illegitimate? Or
Are you one of God's children? The reason I ask this is for
Your own clarification. For though you're a Christian, you still
Can ignore God's chastisement. He will not force on you His will.

Yes for whom the Lord loves, He does chasten, says Hebrews 12:6.
And this verse also says that he "scourges." Sounds harsh, but no, this
Just means "pressure." He'll pressure you, 'til you admit your mistakes.
God is patient. For you to get wiser He's willing to wait.

Read verse seven through ten. We're His children when we can accept
His reproof. Verse eleven says this can be grievous, and yet
Yields the peaceable fruit of His righteousness, all in due time.
It takes time to mature. The rewards of His peace are sublime.

And so how do you know He's correcting you? Often it's when
You are frustrated. Nothing goes right. You're uneasy; on edge.
And so ask yourself, "Am I in error?" You probably know
It already. So do not be stubborn. Let Him help you grow.

What's perceived as Him dogging you, that's your own conscience;
your heart.
If our conscience condemn us, God's greater. He knows every part
Of our thoughts. He knows all things says 1 John verse 3:20. See
It was never God's will for our conscience to guide us; just He.

For your conscience, it only knows "right" verses "wrong," it is not
A good guide. But the hand of God; His Holy Spirit is what,
Rather, Who God wants your guide to be. Hebrews 9 verse fourteen
Says it all; purge your conscience from dead works. Serve Him and be
free.

You won't miss it. Whatever you thought you could not do without;
Whether attitude, things or unwillingness. You'll come about.
And besides just His peace, you'll mature in His holiness. He
Wants you blessed and as healthy and prosperous as you can be.

96 *Meditation*

A mighty verse in the Old Testament is Joshua 1:8.
The Lord Himself told Joshua, on His word he should meditate.
"This book…shall not depart out of thy mouth…" God told him
'speak' the word.
To meditate is speaking to yourself so that you can be heard.

And what would happen if he did this? Well, then he would make his
way
To prosper, and have good success. God's words of life and health
would stay
Within his heart. This would empower him to be a doer of
God's word. For us in the New Testament His laws are faith and love.

This wisdom started in the Old, but the New Testament is where
God's word applies to us. The Covenant of Grace is ours to share
With others. Faith and love, that's what He wants from us. And there
is great
Reward for we who understand the wealth of Joshua 1:8.

The bottom line is: Fix your mind on Him. And in this way, it's You
Who makes your way successful. Focus on His word, and wisdom too.
His benefits and promises you'll know, and you can claim them. See
That having a successful life is your responsibility.

97 *Covenants*

God deals with us through covenants, and you can learn a lot
About the Covenant of Grace, the New, by what is taught
In the Old Testament. The Prophets prophecy about
The Covenant of Jesus' grace; the one we're under now.

Like Daniel and the seventieth week in Daniel 9,
Which tells us in verse twenty-four what God did have in mind.
The everlasting righteousness that we have now because
Of Jesus Christ was prophesied in Daniel. Yes it was.

Let's look at the most often quoted Book, Isaiah. Verse
Eleven of Isaiah 54 shows Jews immersed
In instability; "O thou afflicted, (and thou) tossed
With tempest, and not comforted..." This sounds just like the lost.

So Israel, the nation and its people who had not
Yet entered the New Covenant were troubled by a lot.
But read the rest of verse eleven, and verse twelve. They say,
That, "I (God) will..." do all these pleasant things for you some day.

In verse thirteen Isaiah further prophesies of peace.
Then fourteen does describe this Covenant; oppression's ceased.
"In righteousness shall thou (then) be established..." If you know
That this describes your benefits *right now*, blessed are you so.

The question is, "Are you established in your righteousness?"
Do you know what it means? It means you cannot be oppressed.
It means you're "solid" and you do not waiver. So if you
Have doubts, then you may suffer needless fear and terror too.

It's up to you to straighten out your own head. God has done
All that He's going to do for us. Our righteousness was won
By Jesus Christ. Let Him renew your mind, so you can get
A revelation of His grace and know He paid your debt.

Let's look now at Isaiah 54 verse nine. See how
This Covenant is like the one God made with Noah. Vowed
God never to again destroy the earth with water. He
Swears this time He "would not be wroth…, nor (would) rebuke
(He) thee."

So God is saying that this Covenant, the New, has no
Conditions to it, just like when He made the promise old
With Noah. Read in Genesis verse 9:11, He
Did make a promise that did not depend on men you see.

The rainbow is God's sign that He will never flood again
The earth. His promise, unconditional, does not depend
On man's behavior. Our New Covenant, it is the same.
God will not anger; will not punish us, in Jesus' name.

Isaiah 54 verse ten, God says though mountains and
The hills depart, His kindness, it shall not depart from man.
And, "…neither shall the covenant of my peace be removed…"
Says He whose mercy covers us in righteousness approved.

98 *Grace and Truth*

In John 1:17 we see that "...grace
And truth (they) came by Jesus Christ." Embrace
This knowledge. For the more we think of Him,
The more His grace affects us from within.

Ephesians 1:18 and 19 show
The eyes of your awareness need to grow.
Enlightenment of Him empowers you
To be and do all that He wants you to.

Our eyes of understanding, they can be
In darkness, says Ephesians 4:18.
When ignorance prevails within our minds,
We're cut off from the life of God. We're "blind."

John 1 verse one says Jesus is the "Word."
"Who, being in the form of God..." preferred
To make Himself of reputation none,
So He could be our servant, as God's Son.

Philippians 2:6 and 7 say
This. Further John 1:2 through 4 relay
His fame. Verse nine says Jesus is the true
Light, lighting every man from old to new.

Corinthians the First, 2:9's His word
That "eye (it) has not seen, nor ear (has) heard,
(Nor) entered (in) the heart of man, the things
Which God prepared for (us)." What joy this brings.

To know we're righteous and redeemed is great.
God's love for us, it never fluctuates.
John 1:14 sums up the story of
His grace and truth, and how much we are loved.

99 God's Family

You don't need special qualities to be a member of the most
Inclusive club; God's family. You're good enough. No need to boast
About yourself. God's not impressed. He won't use superstars.
Instead
He uses those who recognize, without Him they're as good as dead.

Yes, Jesus died for all of us. His love extends to everyone.
No matter color, race or creed He welcomes you, excluding none.
Acts chapter 10 relays how God showed Peter, in a dream, that He
Is no respecter of specific persons. We are all redeemed.

When Jesus taught the multitude in chapter 12 of Matthew, He
Was told his mother and his brethren were outside. He then decreed
That whosoever does the will of Father up in heaven, these
Same people are His brother/sister/mother. We're His family.

Paul tells us in Colossians 1 verse twelve, give thanks to Father who
Has made us "meet" (that's "qualified") to be partakers of His true
Inheritance for all the "saints" (believers in Lord Jesus). He
Delivered us from powers of darkness (Satan), teaches verse thirteen.

But more importantly, this verse says God "translated" us into
The kingdom of His Son. Translated means "transformed." We've
been made new.
Corinthians the Second, verse 5:17 confirms that we
Are blessed, because He loves us, and we're part of His great family.

100 *The End*

Let us say that the rapture occurred yesterday. Daniel 9
Twenty-four tells what happens to those who remain. This divine
Revelation was given to Daniel the prophet before
Christ had even been born, indicating God's plan, to be sure.

Note that "Seventy weeks are determined upon (all the Jews)."
Sixty-nine's when Christ died. We are still in between. To ensue
Is the end of this "church" age. When Christians are taken away
Into heaven, the ones left on earth get to suffer that day.

This last "week," (seven years) Tribulation takes place. The first three
And a half years they build a millennial temple, which the
Antichrist desecrates. Then the Jews, still not saved, they do flee
To the mountains where they'll be kept safe supernaturally.

They'll be led by two wings of an eagle. This might be U.S.
And Great Britain? No matter. The end is approaching. Success
Will be Christ's. He'll appear then from heaven, and on that same day
The entire Jewish nation of Israel, all will be saved.

This verse goes on to say, "to (complete) the transgression, and to
Make an end of (all) sins, and make (harmony) for (errors too),
And to bring everlasting (perpetual) righteousness…" We
Have this privilege, as Christians, *right now*. We are righteous indeed!

Made in the USA
Columbia, SC
09 June 2018